GW00541780

Nature's Price. The economics of Mother Earth

WOUTER VAN DIEREN AND
MARIUS G. W. HUMMELINCK

TRANSLATED BY JOYCE E. HOUWAARD-WOOD
EDITED BY JON BARZDO

MARION BOYARS · LONDON · BOSTON

First Published in Great Britain in 1979
by Marion Boyars Publishers Ltd.
18 Brewer Street, London W1R 4AS
and Marion Boyars Inc.
99 Main Street, Salem, New Hampshire 03079
First Published by Het Wereldvenster,
Baarn, Holland, as *Natuur is duur*
Australian distribution by Thomas C. Lothian
4–12 Tattersalls Lane, Melbourne, Victoria 3000.

Printed by Caledonian Graphics Ltd.

ISBN 0 7145 2696 7 hardcover
0 7145 2664 9 paper

Contents

Foreword by Richard Fitter

Foreword

As a conservationist whose sole technical qualification happens to be a degree in economics, I am delighted to be able to commend this book to the English-speaking and English-reading world. For one thing, it shows just how bogus a science classical economics is, with its unrealistic basic assumptions that all human beings are motivated only by greed and that natural resources are inexhaustible and therefore can be taken for granted. Unfortunately all too many human beings are in fact actuated primarily by, if not greed, then an eye to the main chance; and if they are allowed to treat natural resources as inexhaustible, they very soon become exhausted. Witness the historical destruction of the forests of the Mediterranean basin, the quite recent destruction of the plains of 'dustbowl' western North America, and the current rape of the tropical forests of the world. Moreover such rich animal resources as the bison of North America, the great whales of both the northern and southern oceans, and right now the teeming herring stocks of the North Sea, have remorselessly been harvested to near extinction, when common prudence would have suggested that they be conserved for the future use of mankind. Few generations of mankind have cared much for their successors, but the last three or four generations have earned the obloquy of their descendants more thoroughly than most, because the knowledge of the harm they were doing has been there, but they have ignored it.

The authors use a fable – in the correct sense of the word, not its modern meaning of an unlikely tale – of the Island of Terschelling on the Netherlands coast of the North Sea to illustrate their contention that if economic policy treated natural resources – soil, vegetation and animal populations – as an economic good, with a price tag just like artificial man-made goods and services, it would soon become apparent that modern economic policy, made by highly respectable and sober gentlemen in black suits sitting round highly polished tables in centrally heated rooms, resembles nothing so much as the onrush of the swine of Gadara into the sea. As the authors point out, any ordinary housewife or small business man knows that you cannot indefinitely use up your capital without replacing it. And this is just what mankind has been doing, almost since civilisation began. If we were to start now, as is perfectly possible, to set a cash value of natural resources – and the authors tell you how it can be done – this would be the beginning of sanity in economic policy, and perhaps enable economics to make good its arrogant claim to be a science.

The fable ends with a view of Terschelling early in the 21st century, a community in a steady no-growth state, using wind and solar power, and held in balance not by a feudal influence from the top, but by a democracy of equals. Utopia? Maybe, but what other hope is there for the future of mankind than to seek the best in all the warring ideologies rather than embracing any of them whole. And such a state can never come about while society eats away at the natural resources on which ultimately its welfare depends. Earlier civilisations have collapsed for this very reason – there is a strong link between the fall of Rome and the devastation of the Mediterranean forests and grasslands by the suppliers of Rome's sustenance. The eastern and western civilisations of today are the first to start committing suicide in the full knowledge that a way of salvation exists. China has shown signs of knowing what must be done to preserve the material basis of its people's future. There are many in the west – but few of them in positions of power – who know the same. May this book help the good work along.

Richard Fitter
Hon. Secretary
Fauna Preservation Society. London

About This Book

*'God grant me the serenity to accept the
things I cannot change. The courage to
change the things I can, and the wisdom to
distinguish the one from the other'*
                                    Chesterton

This book is the popular version of a report about the value of
nature which was instigated at the request of the Dutch
Branch of the World Wildlife Fund. The plan for this survey
was drawn up by a working party whose chairman was
Marius Hummelinck (the second author). Financial backing
was provided by the Foundation for Pure Scientific Research
and several other benefactors. The study was carried out at
the Amsterdam Institute for Environmental Problems by
Mr. F. Bouma and Dr. S. W. F. van der Ploeg, with the
assistance of seven students.

Our initial aim was simply to find out to what extent the
value of nature could be expressed in money terms. However,
as it turned out there were many more sides to the question.
This led to a closer study of the relationship between the
sciences of economics and ecology.

As it was felt that the scientific reports, which were
produced for use in nature conservation, should be made
available to a wider public, Wouter van Dieren (the first
author) was asked to rewrite them in the form of 'a readable
book, which would also be available to readers in other
countries'.

However, these reports contained so much 'heavy' material, and so much needed to be explained first, that a
completely new piece of work came into existence. So this is
not written as a scientific treatise, nor as a book for specialists

(although we hope they will be interested), but for anyone with an interest in nature or economics. If you read it without being interested, we hope you will become so.

Many people gave us the benefit of their advice from the very beginning of our work. First, our thanks are due to Dr. M. F. Koeman of the Department of Business Administration of the State Agricultural University in Wageningen, Dr. J. H. Westermann, secretary of the World Wildlife Fund, Netherlands and Dr. R. O. Beijdorff of the Foundation for Applied Ecology. Much good advice was also given by Dr. R. Heuting of the Environmental Statistics Branch of the Central Statistical Bureau, Prof. Dr. F. G. Lambooy of the University of Amsterdam, and Prof. Dr. M. F. Mörzer Bruyns of the Department for Nature Conservation of the State Agriculture University, while Dr. F. E. Vermeulen made a study of the influence of man on nature in the island of Terschelling at our request.

One. Apology

Quand une idée simple prend corps, cela fait
une révolution.

Charles Péguy

Nature is our capital. The interest it yields is all we may use.
If we persistently encroach on that capital, we shall eventually go bankrupt. Everybody knows that; from the poli-
tician, administrator and entrepreneur right down to the man
in the street who has his own nest egg. We will refer to this
fact many times. It cannot be overstressed. But we are using
up our natural capital all over the world instead of leaving it
intact, so that not only is nature being wiped out but we are
bringing the same fate upon ourselves.

Anyone who takes the view that nature is capital immediately implies that it has a certain value, and the most
familiar way of expressing value, in these modern times, is by
the standard we call money. In fact, money is nothing but a
handy expedient to help us compare the worth of things of
quite different character. This book is about the value of
nature. We hope that if nature can be defined or assessed by
values which are accepted in economic and political decision-
making (because they fit into existing patterns of thought),
then it will be preserved and respected because of those
values.

If we say that nature has a capital value, it looks as if we
want to hang a price-tag on evolution or, if you like, appraise
God's creation as a piece of merchandise. Or it may appear
that we would like to express the value of life, which is
immeasurable, in terms used for quoting the market prices of

oil, plastic and sun-tan lotion. Even the idea often creates revulsion among dedicated nature-lovers. They believe that the value of nature is inestimable, and that it is absurd to toy with the idea of putting a price on it.

Others simply cannot understand why anyone would ever want to talk about natural capital, and still less why it ought not to be encroached upon. Nature is beautiful enough, but one shouldn't exaggerate. In their eyes, people are no worse off since the dodo (an ugly animal by all accounts) and the auroch ceased to exist. The disappearance of the American passenger pigeon doesn't worry them either. And why should they care about the threatened extermination of the mountain gorilla, the blue whale or the Amazon manatee.

They do not agree with the assumption that nature is so essential, and can see that millions of people live without any contact with nature. 'The new, modern human being makes his own environment and many are quite satisfied with it.' They say they believe that ecological problems (generally meaning pollution) can soon be solved. Technical progress guarantees it. Or does it?

Some scientists are less optimistic. The World Wildlife Fund (WWF) also has little faith in that sort of expertise, if only because not a single living being can be artificially reproduced. And so it is trying to erect a barrier between nature and its attackers. It establishes reserves. It tries to encourage respect for and protection of natural areas and threatened species of animals and plants. It negotiates, promotes research and collects funds with a considerable degree of success. But it is not enough. In spite of all this work, nature is quickly succumbing to great pressures; at least 600 higher species of mammals have died out already and 930 species of animals are known to be on the point of disappearing for ever. According to the results of an investigation published by the University of Hamburg in December 1975, 50,000 species of plants will be eradicated or seriously threatened in the coming twenty five years. At the other end of the scale 240 species of insects, including mites and ticks, are increasing at an alarming rate. DDT and other powerful pesticides no longer have any effect on them. Lice are already resistant in eighteen countries. One of the results of all this is that, in many tropical countries, malaria is occuring on a greater scale than ever before. In Sri Lanka, the number of malaria victims has increased from a few hundred to two million in the last fifteen years. In India in 1975 there were nearly five million, an increase of 30% over 1974. The same thing is happening in Pakistan and densely populated areas of Africa. In these countries, spraying with pesticides has been carried out on such a large scale that the fine-mesh of relationships between plants, animals and their environment has been ruined; nature has been thrown out of balance and with far too heavy a burden has ceased to perform its protective function.

Sometimes, though, nature conservationists do win a victory. Nature reserves are established and endangered species saved in the nick of time. But these new items reach the papers because they are so exceptional, and not because they are the rule. When we read these pieces of good news, we tend to forget what has been lost somewhere else that same day.

Some people are less passive and conduct campaigns: WWF, International Union for Conservation of Nature, United Nations Environmental Programme, Friends of the Earth, Audubon Society, Sierra Club, Greenpeace and many other organizations and action-groups. Admittedly, much of this is rearguard action, because they are fighting losing battles. If they stop to consider their true position, they must be filled with fear and despair.

There is a growing feeling in these organizations that something is wrong with the standards used to measure progress and prosperity. This does not mean we use only philosophic meditations, religious experiences or ethical rules to weigh up the many kinds of values in our civilisation; we can still use the economic principles which are internationally accepted. People seem habitually to choose the wrong course to reach their goal. We seem to be aiming at a prosperity which deserves that name less and less, because it is at the expense of nature, of the environment, and so of ourselves. The lighthouses have been erected in the wrong place, and before people realize it, they are on the rocks. Our biggest mistake is in our method of calculating. Prosperity is treated as an addition sum, and nature's contribution is forgotten. What is even worse, items deducted from nature are entered as assets. The loss inflicted on essential sources of life, such as water, soil, air, forests and marshes, are *added* to the measure of prosperity which is called the Gross National Product. And this is the main reason why so many people believe they are benefitting from their exploitation of nature.

We live in a maze of figures: times, speeds, market prices, rates of interest, statistics, growth percentages, building capacity, lotteries, football results, taxes, birth rates, death rates, investments, mortgages, Gross National Product and National Income. Figures, figures, figures.. . . But the consequence is that figures seem to be almost the only way in which very many values can be expressed. Eventually people got on to the wrong track with all this figuring and forgot, for example, that it is not the *amount* of the national income which is important but what we mean to express by it: the quality of existence, how healthy and contented a population is.

Even in schools, subjects such as biology, history and geography are becoming increasingly mathematical or giving way to those subjects which are. The foundation for these latest changes was laid in the nineteen fifties, when progress in the development of computers was so crucial. People were quick to believe that the future would be decided by the computer and they started to adapt the curriculum to it throughout the industrialized west.

Biology is the study of living nature, history the study of past events and geography is the science of space. Space, history and nature determine our existence to a large extent and we can understand a lot about them by measuring their dimensions. But anyone who lays any significance in the figures themselves forgets that they are only a means of helping us to express observations and relationships in the world around us more clearly. The tragedy of the future is that a generation is growing up divorced from this knowledge of relationships. A generation which, sadly, needs that knowledge more than any before it.

When we see a film, inhale perfume, drive a car or sit in an armchair, the feelings we experience can also be expressed in figures in a roundabout way as a price, for the goods creating those feelings are *produced* by people, are offered, and are consumed. And we take it for granted that if we want to experience the feeling of *looking* at a play, *driving* a car, *relaxing* in an armchair or *smelling* perfume, we must pay the price. *But as soon as such feelings can be experienced freely through nature*, people object at any attempt to place a monetary value on them. Yet this is an irrational reaction. For we are still talking about personal pleasures, but in this case they come from *looking* at nature, *driving* through the countryside, *relaxing* on the banks of a stream or inhaling fresh air. So we *do* accept that goods produced by man have a price, but cannot see that the 'goods' of nature, obtained free, and satisfying the same needs, also have a value (or a price). The *price* is a measure of the value which people give to goods. This value varies from zero to infinity, depending on one's lifestyle and priorities and on the availability of the goods; that is, on supply and demand. Generally, where there is a great demand, a small supply means a high price, and vice versa. Therefore the price reflects the market value. Although many people believe it debases nature to consider it in the same way as a piece of merchandise, we intend to show that it has just as great a contribution to make to prosperity as goods of all kinds produced by human means (and the latter often at the expense of nature). If we can prove this, then we can compare the value of those natural functions with that of ordinary consumer goods which have a recognized price and to which roughly the same importance can be attached. For example. a lake can purify a certain amount of organic waste. Its 'purification value' expressed in money, is therefore comparable with the cost of a technical installation of the same purification capacity. In this way we can try to estimate the contribution which nature makes to prosperity.

If a man produces a useless product nobody buys it and it is taken off the market. But people often imagine that a product of nature has no value, because they do not know what function it fulfills. Our aim is to prevent the product 'nature' from being taken off the market because of this lack of understanding. We do not suggest for a moment that areas of nature be sold as merchandise, but it is important to make its value clear to politicians, administrators, entrepreneurs and all those who make decisions affecting the well-being of the natural environment. 'Investment' means conservation and care; and 'yield' is health, safety and an assured future. When deciding what to do with a piece of ground or water, our system rarely gives any thought to the possibility of leaving it untouched. Similarly, the harm caused to nature and even to humans by over-exploitation, pollution or disturbance, has hardly ever been considered.

All this will have to change, and all the interests, which often clash, must be weighed up. Which has priority? Is it housing? Traffic? Industry? Agriculture? Or perhaps nature?

Up to now, nature has come off rather badly, because its real value was either not accepted or not understood. And we must be more careful about weighing things up. Not only should the creation of jobs and other benefits be taken into account, but so should the injurious effects which building, traffic and industry have on nature and the environment, and on both sides of the scale we must take the future into consideration. Perhaps we shall then reach a completely new kind of economy. One in which industrial production will have a place, if only because the world cannot manage without it. But any production *will* be in accord with nature's part in prosperity.

Much will have been won if those in charge of the scales can be made to see which considerations weigh most heavily. If they can be brought to realize that nature, too, should be looked on as capital, then this book will have succeeded in its purpose. It will then be obvious that nature's capital should be preserved just like that of industry or of a bank or state. And if this does not happen . . .?

The conservation of wildlife is largely dependent on the amount of space that people are willing to leave. Aldous Huxley wrote *Brave New World* in 1932. Paul Ehrlich wrote *Eco-Catastrophe* in 1969. Signs indicate that they saw the future with alarming perspicacity. In many countries, nature only exists behind wire fences. The first plastic roadside vegetation is with us already in Los Angeles and Avignon. Even the trees are replaced by prosaic concrete structures. Plastic gardens, with trees, bushes, grass, flowers and moss all made from synthetic materials are found in Arizona and New Mexico. Even arts, which have immortalized and honoured animals and plants for centuries are becoming more and more divorced from nature. The famous painter Vasarely proclaims 'It's time we stopped concerning ourselves with romantic nature! *Our* nature is biochemistry, mechanics, . . . and astronomy. Let us realize that all human creation is tied up in geometric structures, just as the universe is . . .'

The sculptor and painter Constant, who created the 'society of the future' called New Babylon, goes even further. He has a fully automated future in mind, where man has to give scope to his supreme creativity in roofed-in urban structures, kilometres long: air-conditioned, mechanized, a robot society. Nature plays no part in New Babylon. The production of energy in this (thankfully) imaginary society is so great that every part of the natural environment is destroyed. Not that this presents any problem for the New Babylonians. They belong to a human type which, in Constant's philosophy, has nothing to do with ecology or wildlife.

Not only is this kind of vision ethically abhorrent, it is also impossible in practice, Every human being is bound to the living environment by an unbreakable network of biological and physical threads. So we can forget the idea of a New Babylon.

The decision-makers of today's society must be made aware that there are things happening now which will make them an abomination to generations unborn. Who are these decision-makers? How do their minds work? How do they judge priorities? How do they finally reach a decision?

They think in figures, in money. They estimate investments and interests and are financially responsible to those for whom they work. They know that 'politics is the organisation of the possible'. Their activities are limited by what electors, supporters, stockholders, bankers and unions allow them to do. As a rule, allowances will be made on the basis of what the figures say. Their greatest incentive is always 'economic growth', which really means increased production, commercial growth or financial growth. So it has been for centuries past in the developed world. And so it will continue, *until* we can make it very plain that nature, too, is a part of the economy and its health is an essential condition for our prosperity.

Some people are convinced that nature and the environment can only be saved by drastic changes in the structure of society, and this is sometimes taken to mean that free enterprise should be abolished. What they really object to is the fact that making a profit is usually, if not always, the prime objective in free enterprise, so the nature of the goods produced becomes of secondary importance. The target is greater production and lower costs, often at the expense of the environment. The supposition is that a concern belonging to only one, or a few people, is a greater threat to the environment and community than an undertaking run collectively by the workers, or by the state. It remains to be seen whether this is true. Perhaps one day there will be people who run an enterprise in a new, democratic way, respecting nature. If this ever comes about, much will have gained, but the situation is so serious now that the conservationist cannot wait around for things to happen.

When a fire breaks out, only the fire extinguisher is important. Discussions about building a fireproof house (which would have been the ideal) can only take place later. Otherwise the ideal would be the enemy of the 'best at the time'. In this book, we are looking for 'the best at the time'.

Our starting point is that our world is a patchwork of imperfect forms of society, and that it will remain so for the time being.

The great mistake which western man makes in his dealings with nature relates to the development of the natural sciences. 'Knowing by measuring' has assumed enormous importance because, in research, *objects and processes can be isolated from their surroundings*. Only by eliminating as many influences as possible could specific properties come to light. This has become common practice. Theoretical and isolated plans have led to many unforeseen side-effects when put into effect. The natural sciences have – in spite of their name – almost invariably restricted themselves to the study of phenomena in dead matter. Even biology is studied more in the laboratory than in the field. The way in which a phenomenon is studied has often been limited to that which could be determined quantitatively. Until the end of the last century, there was a commonly-held opinion that there was no place for a science which tried to explain the phenomena of the organic world, i.e. of nature.

What we do know about the secret of life is so little that it will take a long time before nature's role is taken into account in our plans as a matter of course. In the meantime we should seize every opportunity to express the value of nature in 'economic' terms. Maybe the time will come when nature's value, as essential for prosperity as well as for its beauty, is realized.

This foreword then, is more than an argument, it is also an apology to those who think nature is insulted by the application of financial values.

Two. The Island: World Problems on a Small Scale

'We cannot command nature except by obeying her'
Francis Bacon in *Novum Organum*

The island of Terschelling is situated at the furthest point north-west of Europe, where storms come howling round the coast and drive the waves on to dash themselves against the cliffs of Denmark and Norway. Indeed, the trees lean sideways because of the prevailing westerly wind. It is a very old island, visited in earliest times by Irish monks who have left their mark. The massive lighthouse, which pierces the night with its powerful beam, radiating far over the ground-swells on the salty horizon, still bears the name of St. Brendan, their famous leader. Treasure seekers find stones, silver objects and bones belonging to those seafarers, who left their tokens on all the coasts of the north Atlantic: tombstones, little churches, ruins and hills full of mystery, waiting for the first spade. And there is a remarkable history to this island. Famous men roved the sea and left their names behind in world history. They were victors or vanquished in sea-battles, captains of the fleets of Holland or Friesland, intruders into England, or simply those whiling away the winter in the polar night. They were simple but by no means God-fearing fishermen, farmers or artisans, creating a local culture behind the large white sand dunes and a low, green dyke.

The island is not large, no more than thirty kilometres by six, and the 4,000 people there inhabit less than half of it, in about ten rather attractive villages and hamlets. In spring, the

sand-coloured gables and red tiles of the houses make a
shining contrast with the fresh green tints of the vegetation,
the richest in north-west Europe. In the warm days of
summer, these colours become powdered with dust. Then the
high farmhouse roofs, which reach nearly to the ground,
appear lazy and sleek in the scorching countryside. In the
short days and stormy nights of autumn and winter, these
identical roofs look like protective palms of the hand pressed
down to keep its wards snugly sheltered from the cruel forces
rolling up out of the west, cold, stormy and wet.

This ground marks the northern boundary of that vast
unbelievable waterscape called the Wadden; extending from
the tip of north Holland along the coasts of Friesland,
Germany and Schleswig-Holstein right up to Denmark. A
refuge for millions of birds, a spawning ground for just as
many fishes and a breeding place for billions of other
organisms; shellfish, worms, snails, crabs and many more. It
is neither sea nor land, neither marsh nor sandbank, but has
something in common with all of them. The islanders built a
dyke between the Wadden and the lowlands behind the
dunes, which had formed on the sandbanks thousands of
years ago. But the eastern part of the island is still unpro-
tected, and twice in every twenty four hours the sea ripples
through the channels, depressions and ditches and flows deep
into the level areas. The water streams in between the dunes,
leaving food for a flora and fauna whose richness is hardly
equalled anywhere on the continent. To the north of the
range of dunes lies the North Sea, blue and inviting in
summer, grey, repellent and leaden in autumn and winter.
Masts of sunken ships reach out from the breakers, but never
for long. Within a few years, wind and water bury even the
largest vessels under layers of sand many metres deep. In the
waves there still lies gold from an English naval ship which
foundered here in the eighteenth century. Only a few thousand bars were ever recovered. The sunken vessels supply the
island with wood. The beams of many a farmhouse once
swayed as yardarms above the sails of ships now forgotten.
Piles were hammered in, sheds built, waggons and sleds

constructed, all from the wood which has supplied beach-combers for centuries. In the depressions between the dunes, the American cranberry grows, washed ashore a long time ago and seeming quite at home in this alien territory. But butter, whiskey and port were washed up as well, enough to provide the entire population with food and drink for years. And if ever times were hard, a fire on a dune top was sufficient to deceive a seafarer, so that his ship went off course, ran aground, surrendering its crew, hull and cargo to the waves. That, however, is a gory page in the history of their existence which is mostly filled with prosperity, unity, and the harmony of good-neighbourliness, festivity and tradition.

In the middle of the island there stands a mill. Less than twenty years ago, farm carts used to drive to and fro, loaded with rye, oats and barley. They were drawn by proud Friesian horses, jet black with broad hooves, long stockings and manes. A smell of meal filled the air in the neighbourhood, where the quiet was only disturbed in the heart of summer by the sea, the crying of gulls, the clucking of hens and a thud of hooves with the crunching of cartwheels on the shell path: if there was a wind, there was also the swishing of the mill sails and the rumble of millstones and wooden wheels. There was a wooden chute for getting the sacks of flour from the first gallery to the ground floor. It was worn mirror-smooth by years of use and, when the miller was not grinding grain, the children who lived round about would use it as a slide. Their trousers and shirts were white, but they knew where bread came from, and not everyone can say as much today. The milk-collector came twice a day, a farmer's son whose speech was as slow as the steps of his horse. The children used to ride along with him from one farm to the next, and the full milk churns were delivered to the dairy factory. Cheese was made there, and it lay motionless in the vats of brine.

In the evenings, the farming folk would go dancing. On the mainland, people thought you had 'a touch of the sun' if you ever spoke with appreciation of those islanders who sang and danced to the music of a concertina and violin, like the generations before them. Folkdancing was considered arcadian, not 'with it', and might as well disappear, sacrificed to whatever progress had to offer in its place.

The islanders, unaware of this opinion, would sing and dance unperturbed, with a solidarity expressed in sounds and celebrated in herb gin. They loved all this merry-making. When the day's work was over or a willing neighbour was prepared to carry out the most necessary chores, horses were harnessed to the covered waggons, bottles were stowed away and the food hampers filled. Then they would set off in procession to an open meadow between the dunes, halting at many culverts. Nobody knew why they stopped in those particular places but tradition called for a certain song at each, and a prescribed number of raised glasses. Eventually the – by now, slightly tipsy – procession would arrive at the meadow, where the horses were unharnessed and dancing started. It could go on for hours, until the lengthening shadows forced them to turn homewards and, in the falling dusk, they would drive back to the villages at a walking pace. Lanterns lit up the tired and sweaty faces, and the mouths – less raucous now – went on humming the old, traditional songs, the sound gradually diminishing as more people got off at every bend in the road to end the day at their front door.

This ideal community lived in equilibrium with the nature that surrounded it. Protection against the wind was found in earth banks planted with bushes surrounding meadows and farmyards. If a cow became ill it was put to graze in the finest natural meadows, whose varied vegetation we now know to be responsible for the sick cow's recovery. Grateful use was made of winter floods, because they meant fertilization and were the natural condition for the cultivation of highly-prized cranberries. Cultivation and nature got along well together and hardly anyone was poor or needy. If ever there was mismanagement – and it did happen from time to time – its limited extent was the reason why no more damage was done than could be put right again.

There is no harmony now. At the beginning of this century technical civilization began to spread its influence here. Since

then, the island's natural resources have been gradually
destroyed, a little at a time. Later, what is called 'economic
growth' secured a hold on the island so that the disintegration
process speeded up. This is especially significant, because it is
situated on the rim of one of the last great tidal areas of the
world (declared by the World Wildlife Fund to be one of its
important projects). It is an area where nature and man are
trying in vain to live in harmony with one another.

It began as a narrow strip grown up on a ridge of sand in the
coastal sea, and extensive marshes developed behind it. More
than a thousand years ago, the first inhabitants came to that
sandy ridge, where they fished, hunted, and gradually began
to defend their territory against the sea. The sandy ridge grew
higher, areas of wild meadowland evolved, and the dunes
started to pile up. Then, about 400 years ago, a dyke was built
limiting the advance of the sea. Yet it was not a truly man-
made area; human influence was too slight for this and the
power of nature too great. The people kept their hands off
nature, except for managing the polder and the dykes, and
occasionally being too rapacious. There was fishing and
shipping and, in the seventeenth and eighteenth centuries,
whaling introduced a period of material prosperity. When the
maritime activities started to disappear, this important source
of income also dried up – at the end of the last century. There
was little to do apart from farming. Population growth was at
a standstill, and any increase in income would not be feasible
for many decades.

In the year 1900, the state of the island was as we have
described it. Harmonious, unspoiled, and possessing a beauty
which is now unimaginable. What happened between 1900
and 1975 is known in detail. Several reports on the economic
state of the island have been produced. Nature has been
observed, admired, displayed as a tourist commodity, misused and trampled underfoot. Its downfall has accompanied
the rise of industry and tourism. In 1975, the population had
the highest income per head of the three northern provinces
of the Netherlands – a prosperity whose end is not yet in sight.
So why should it come to an end? The people are wealthy and

the tourist industry flourishes as never before.

But the first signs of decay are visible. As recently as 1959, it was written that nature here 'is still comparatively well-off; far away from industry; clean sea wind'. In 1971 we read, however, that there is industrial pollution in the rain; this includes nitrogen, chlorine and nitrate compounds, emanating from Dutch and German industry, and also coming from England and Belgium. Most people will shrug their shoulders at the thought of such a small amount of chemical waste matter. But nature is sensitive to slight disturbances. Nitrogen compounds enrich the underground water, so that higher plant species are enabled to spread more rapidly at the expense of simple plants, such as the mosses and lichens. These, however, are more important than the layman imagines. The mosses – known to the dune-walker as greyish, dry, spongy ground cover – are important colonisers of the dune slopes. These lower species help to bind the dune surface together so that the higher plants can grow there. But, if the colonising species disappear, the surface becomes vulnerable to rain and wind and the chance of drifting increases. A small cause – a serious consequence.

Until 1900, one could see no signs of human influence on the dunes and beaches. Beachcombers and rescuers came along, but their visits did not have any negative influence on form and vegetation; certainly not when compared with the natural influences of sea, wind, temperature, precipitation, and minerals in the ground. Dunes, beaches and tidal marshes have therefore been able to develop undisturbed into a region with a rich variety of plants and animals, that is rare in this part of Europe. The mid-dune area – a wide strip of dunes between the margin of the sea and the meadowlands on the south side – was, however, used intensively for many kinds of economic purposes. Practically everything which the sun converted here into plant growth or animal life was put to use, especially in periods when the income from trade and shipping had decreased to some extent. Marram grass, sea buckthorn, creeping willow, bog myrtle and other plants served as fuel; marram grass was used for rope and lashings, rushes as pith for lamp wicks, centaury for medicine, bog-myrtle went to the brewery and the 'more palatable' green plants were for the small livestock. Seaweed was fished up off the coast, spread out to dry on the dyke and used for stuffing mattresses. Finally, shell-fishing was a source of income from a very early date. The shells were sold to road builders and for use in limekilns.

The intensive use of the mid-dune area depleted the dune flora and led to erosion. The dunes shifted still further into the polder; then in 1880 a farm called 'De Kooi' had become so smothered in sand that it had to be demolished. The dunes became so bare through the excessive gathering of plants that drifting resulted and some dunes shifted as much as one to two kilometres. It was anything but a harmonious association with nature, for even such small-scale activities as gathering dead wood and collecting flowers can lead to such fantastic results as shifting sand dunes. What happened here in a small way is a scale model of the world problem; over-exploitation leads to erosion and the ultimate result is hunger and poverty.

At the beginning of this century the island had its first streets made. A sandy track fourteen km. long was transformed into a metalled road; a gasworks and, later, a small power station were built and the first tourists arrived. All of which greatly benefitted the inhabitants, while the impact on nature was not yet great, though its character has changed very much compared with that of the nineteenth century.

In 1977, hardly anything survives of the character in 1900. In most areas the natural environment has been seriously injured by human influence. Only in a few places has the influence had any positive effect, so that nature has flourished there. We shall see later that the overall effect is ultimately a detrimental effect on prosperity, income and the population.

In assessing the results of seventy-five years of human interference with the island's natural resources, we find that the beach and adjacent dunes now have to cope with 140,000 tourists annually; in the summer of 1908, there were 250. The dune vegetation is being trampled flat everywhere, birds are disturbed and, though breeding grounds are patrolled, the birds are restless. The beach, which used to be littered with wood from ships, is seriously polluted, although this is not entirely the tourists' fault. The effect of glass and oil, plastic and other indestructable rubbish, is that the beach now bears little resemblance to an area of nature. The smallest slivers of wood used to be seized for the stove: now they are left on the beach. There are barbed wire entanglements, parking places, hotels and holiday cottages. The once strictly natural coastal protection measures now include planting with reeds and marram grass, and work is carried out by bulldozers and other mechanical means. Yet one can still call the area a natural one on the whole although it has obviously deteriorated since 1900.

What has had the effect of positively enriching nature has been the building of dykes to impede sand-drifting. They dam up the over-dynamic influences of wind and sea and help create areas for wildlife in their lee, which are more important than what existed there before. This extra natural wealth brought other human influences along with it, hitherto unknown. The island is haunted by bird watchers, scientific researchers and, above all, holiday makers. So many of the latter, indeed, that those looking for peace, and bird watchers are hard put to it to find that peace, and the birds.

The mid-dune area, which was so heavily plundered last century, has been affected more radically. It is true that positive steps have been taken. For example, cattle are no longer allowed to wander freely through the dunes: this custom could have led to total erosion. Because electricity, coal and gas became available, plants were no longer used for fuel and the natural vegetation could spread. In addition, some recreational provisions made it possible for the number and variety of plants to increase.

An important step was the decision to afforest parts of this area. There have never been woodlands there; the decision was taken because it was supposed that forests would help to stabilize the dunes. Additional motives were the provision of employment and even timber production. Forests give variety to the landscape, provide windbreaks and attract songbirds. But they also had disadvantages for the island because they brought about changes in the natural biological process, which have not yet worked themselves out. Consider how important this fact is: the upheaval which afforestation caused has had effects which are still being felt more than fifty years later!

When trees are planted on the island, shallow trenches are dug first in the dunes, by which means the underground water level can be lowered. The dune area dries up and many species of plants disappear. The heath vegetation gives way to imported, cultivated varieties of conifers, which create an acid, poor, humus layer, so that very little of the previously rich dune vegetation is left. The plantations lead to an explosion of the rabbit population, which has to be reduced. In the new system of channels and trenches, required by the woods, the water vole also breeds at an amazing rate. It gnaws away underground at the roots of young trees and plants and undermines the dunes, and is supported in this destructive activity by the rabbits. In order to contend with the water-voles, their predatory enemies, such as hedgehogs, stoats and weasels, were imported. Between 1909 and 1924, 44,013 water-vole tails were handed in by the premium-conscious people. The stoats and weasels disposed of the water-voles for good in less than six years, but then became a problem themselves. Weasels were no match for stoats, and died out. The stoats prey on rabbits, chickens, ducks and even on birds on the beach and in the water.

Everything is now in a state of flux. Each step taken creates another problem. In no time, nature is in such a state of confusion that disturbances and plagues are common-place. Sometimes, fire is used to fight caterpillars which have established themselves in the dune vegetation, but this only leads to an increase in their number because their natural enemies perish in the flames. Because of the increasing numbers of holiday-makers, roads and paths are constructed and all kinds of birds and plants disappear.

When land was re-allocated (in 1949) the semi-natural grasslands of the polder, where some very rare orchids used to grow, were converted into modern grazing lands with fixed boundaries. These grazing lands soon lost their wealth of plant species, because of the use of chemical pesticides. Nature disappeared from the polder, and it became a modern agricultural landscape. An incipient industrialization made matters worse; waste water was discharged, causing the polder water to become polluted and, as a result, a few dominant plant species drove out the old varied vegetation.

Farmers had a hard struggle to make ends meet in the face of industrial development and the European agricultural policy, and could not hold out for long. One after another, they gave up and moved to the tourist industry in catering for campers and other such jobs. Only the commercial farmers with very large areas could manage to keep their heads above water. So plots of land were joined together to make bigger fields, new metalled roads built, and large, ugly milking parlours built. When the old farming community died out, the old ways went with them. In less than twenty five years (between 1950 and 1975), the annual invasion of tourists has eliminated all that was characteristic of the indigenous population. Sociological research has shown that the islanders have lost their social stability along with their agricultural way of life. This is illustrated by a sharp rise in petty crime, alcoholism, divorce and other symptoms of disintegration.

But the islanders are rich; no doubt about that. So they live in a tourist playground, with nature dying all around them, are said to be socially disorganized (which makes them burst out laughing), and they are happily thinking that prospects are bright.

Probably, they are wrong. Their income is based on part of the natural capital, the 'Island Product', which they sell to the holiday-maker. But, without realising it, they have encroached on that capital itself, and as every economist can tell you, that is the easiest way to go bankrupt. The process is demonstrated by the graph on p. 22

The unbroken line indicates the amount of 'recreation industry' with the resulting income which has developed

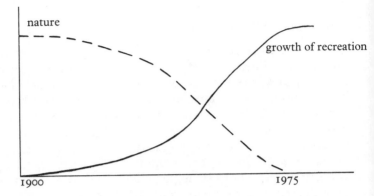

since 1900. By 1975 the considerable growth had not yet reached its peak. The dotted line shows the wealth of nature. When the growth of recreation begins there is a great deal of unspoiled nature but as it increases the wealth of nature decreases. And the price we pay for the process of economic growth is the destruction of our wildlife heritage.

That one profits from another's loss is one of those rules inherent in every economic process, but rarely concerns anyone because the supplies of raw materials, nature, cheap labour, and space have always been thought plentiful – until fairly recently. What is happening on our island is happening all over the world. Many a famous country or seaside resort has lost its old glory and the residents wonder greatly why the continuous growth of their community does not lead any more to prosperity, not to mention happiness.

On the small scale of our island it is easier to see what the future holds for an industry like recreation, which is squandering its own capital. Recreation will go on increasing for some time to come, because there is a certain lag-effect in its growth. It can be compared with the mass of a car which keeps on travelling for many metres after the brakes have been slammed on. The bosses of the island's recreation industry will have their minds set at ease by that effect. All will appear well, with the tourists still queueing up for the 'Island Product' and they will carry on as before. Constructing roads, admitting cars, building hotels, driving birds away and eradicating plants. But in the long run this attitude is unrealistic. When its mass is no longer impelled forward, the car eventually comes to a stop. What the visitors seek on the island is not only the shops, hotels, midget-golf courses, chip stalls and souvenir shops created by the industry but above all the Product of nature, For that is what makes the island unique and decides its market value. If it is destroyed, the island will have to compete with scores of similar tourist places, and the market advantage which it owed to nature will be lost.

The result will be a rapid drop in the number of visitors and so of income, until the pressure on nature is lessened and it can begin to recover. Unfortunately this process will take very many decades.

However, gradually more people are becoming aware of that danger. From the 1973 structure plan for the future one can conclude that the authorities intend to limit the tourist industry to a level and character that nature can tolerate. This does not mean a return to poverty, which everyone is afraid of, but a stabilization of the economic structure which is simultaneously brought into balance with nature. It has been proved that stabilization also means greater social rest than accompanies the present expanse of production. Social calm *and* nature restored mean a more harmonious community, with a greater resemblance to that which was lost. A fairy tale which, on the isle of Terschelling, may still come true.

Terschelling . . . an island at peace.

above The Indian elephant. Will it disappear as
below the Aepyornis and Dodo, hunted until extinct

Three. Vanishing Nature

'What is man without the beasts? If all the beasts were gone, men would die from a great loneliness of spirit. For whatever happens to the beasts happens to man. All things are connected'.

Chief Seattle, 1854

The comparison of our island's changes with those occurring internationally is not merely hypothetical, for nature is suffering the same fate all over the world. Increasing material prosperity on the one hand goes with destruction on the other. On the one hand is mankind. And on the other is wildlife, in its natural habitat.

The disappearance of countless species of plants and animals cannot be prevented merely by a sort of technical first-aid, although some optimists think this will be the solution to our pollution problems. Indeed, we can obtain clean water and clean air like this providing that we don't wait too long, for then the so called 'law of increasing misery' will start operating again. Roughly, this law says that pollution increases in proportion to the increase of production and the use of energy. When the pollution is tackled by technical means, this again requires production and energy, resulting in a spiral: problem → technical solution → problem, etc.

Technology is useful, but is not an all-embracing solution, however. In any case, it is impossible to reconstruct plants which have disappeared or animals which are extinct. Many of these have disappeared without the aid of man. There were other reasons, such as climatic changes or natural competition. So, they were not exterminated but died out naturally. One example is the brontosaurus, an enormous prehistoric monster, though it was small when compared with the blue whale and other large cetaceans now being massacred by means of radar and harpoon guns. The brontosaurus died out because the climate changed, so that its food became scarce, or because its eggs were eaten by new species of small mammals. The mammoth probably disappeared because it was overtaken by the ice age.

But since the coming of man (and especially in the last hundred years), and because of him, the impoverishment of nature has increased alarmingly. That everything might have been much worse is nonsense. The World Wildlife Fund recently published a list of nearly a thousand 'higher' animals which are in danger of being exterminated. This list, printed in small type, is nearly three metres long and includes 297 species of mammals, 359 birds, 187 reptiles and 79 species of fish. Less is known about the numbers of plants which are threatened, but the 50,000 previously mentioned is a reasonable estimate and would make a list 120 metres long.

Disappearing animals

The giant panda, the symbol of the World Wildlife Fund, has got off comparatively lightly. There were never very many of them, and the present population lives well-protected in the bamboo forests of the Chinese province of Szechwan, in the Wang Lang reserve in the Min Chan mountains. Their only enemy there is the leopard. In 1869, the French Jesuit, Père Armand David, was the first to discover the pelt of an unknown black and white 'bear', found in a country house belonging to a mandarin of high rank. The animal very soon became the target of fanatical scientists, zoo proprietors and hunters. On 13 April 1929, Kermit and Theodore Roosevelt, sons of the President of the United States, were the first western hunters to shoot a specimen. In 1939, the then Chinese government gave full protection to the panda, although hunts have taken place since that time, especially because many zoos were eager to possess specimens.

Most of the birds of prey native to western Europe and parts of North America have already disappeared from those areas. Hundreds of millions of songbirds die of poison or lack of food or because they are mercilessly trapped for food in Italy and France. Of the formerly very rich fauna in the industrial areas of the world, little more than scavengers and insects will survive, together with those few species which have adapted, such as crows, sea gulls, sparrows, mice and rats. Nor does man spare even his nearest relations. Our natural cousin, the orang-utan, is one of the most threatened primates. Orang-utans are only found in north Sumatra and Borneo, where tree-felling and hunting are reducing both their numbers and their habitat. The wild caught adults often pine away in captivity and in any case are difficult to catch, so the mother animal is killed and its young sold, fetching up to £3,430 (8,000 dollars) each in 1978. In the Gunung Leuser reserve in Sumatra, the World Wildlife Fund is trying to teach young animals, found in the possession of poachers and private individuals, how to fend for themselves again in the wild.

The mountain gorilla lives in only a few mountainous areas of Central Africa, mainly in Rwanda and Zaïre. Few more than five hundred still survive. Their number is declining rapidly as a result of human interference in their habitat. One reason is that part of that habitat is very suitable for the cultivation of pyrethrum (a plant from which a vegetable pesticide is made), and for bananas.

The Sumatran rhinoceros lives not only in Sumatra but also in Borneo, Malaya, Burma and Thailand. Like all rhinoceroses, its misfortune is that its nasal ornament provides the raw materials for an Eastern aphrodisiac which is in great demand. Wealthy orientals especially, with many wives but little potency, are willing to pay enormous sums for it. So this species seems doomed. The World Wildlife Fund and the Indonesian government are also trying to save the last few dozen smaller, Javan rhinoceroses in the Udjung Kulon reserve in Java. But the limited population gives little cause for hope at present.

The 'kings' of nature too, the great felines, have a decreased life-expectancy. Too many women prefer to see the leopard as a coat on their backs than in the wild where it belongs. The leopard (or panther) is found in Indonesia, Indo-China, over much of Southern Asia and throughout Africa, but in spite of being so widely distributed, its chances of survival are not great, and in many places it has already been exterminated.

Of the various races of the tiger, the Indian tiger can still perhaps be saved from extinction. The World Wildlife Fund is campaigning for this. Of the other races, such as the Siberian, Chinese, Indo-Chinese, Caspian and Sumatran tigers, only scattered remnants still survive. The Bali tiger is extinct and, according to latest reports, there are only five Javan tigers left, so these too can be written off. The skins of spotted cats are not only made into fur coats but are used on boots and as covers for car seats and transistor radios. And, of course, their habitat too is rapidly disappearing.

The dreaded crocodiles, which threatened travellers in many a fantastic tale and throng the banks of romantic rivers, are very scarce nowadays. Years ago, it was a great fight to capture one with a spear or a simple gun and you had to be sure of hitting the right spot, but firearms have become more efficient and the demand for crocodile skins for handbags, coats and souvenirs is still high.

For a long time the status of the great American 'buffalo' (actually a bison) was very precarious. In the 18th century, 600 million of them roamed over the vast prairies. By 1830, the number had dwindled to 20 million as a result of indiscriminating hunting, and then things speeded up. The bison were almost completely wiped out partly for their meat and skins, but especially because shooting them was such tremendous fun. When the great railroads to the West were being built, food was needed for the workmen. The most important supplier of meat was William Cody, alias Buffalo Bill, who brought down 4,280 buffalos. Hundreds of thousands of them were shot without mercy and without any reason. There were special trains run for the Sunday hunters. Sitting on their leather seats in the train, a glass of whiskey within reach, they would fire away to their hearts' content. At times the train could go no further, because the line was blocked by the rotting pile of flesh from a previous pleasure trip. The hundreds of vultures and coyotes ignored the stench, and clouds of flies darkened the air and found their way into the train through every nook and cranny. In 1894 there were still about 1100 bison left and the last small group was finally given protection in Yellowstone Park. By 1920, their numbers had begun to build up again. Now some tens of thousands graze there, most of them rightly in the wild. Luckily this regal animal was saved from destruction in the nick of time.

However, the zebra-wolf or Tasmanian wolf, a predator from Australia and Tasmania, may no longer survive. We do not know. It could not compete with the dingo (a feral dog introduced by early aborigines) and was also hunted by man for its reputation as a sheep killer. An expedition set out to find specimens in 1940 and was unsuccessful. A few paw prints, presumed to be of the wolf, were seen in 1956, and a dubious sighting was reported early in 1978. How ironic it is that, although the Tasmanian wolf was probably exterminated long ago, it is now protected by law.

The dodo – exterminated. The aurochs – exterminated. The flightless cormorant – threatened. The musk-ox, Asian lion, the Californian condor and the white crane – threatened. The African and Indian elephant – threatened. The north African dama gazelle – almost extinct. In common with many other species of gazelles, these swift-footed animals were run down with jeeps until they fell exhausted, then were shot: so they were wiped out.

The Galapagos hawk – threatened. The woodpecker finch, the peregrine falcon, the sea eagle, the frigate bird, the gannet, the sandwich tern, etc., etc.

Photosynthesis and food chains

At the beginning of all life there is a process called carbonic acid assimilation or photosynthesis. By this process solar energy is converted into a form which can be used by living creatures. Photosynthesis can only take place in the green specks of chlorophyll which are present in plants, including some microscopically small algae. In chemical reaction water and carbon dioxide from the air are converted into glucose. Oxygen is released, and given off into the atmosphere as a gas. Photosynthesis is just the beginning of an endless series of conversions, which take place in the thin layer of atmosphere surrounding the earth called the biosphere. Cellulose, starch and other carbon compounds are formed from the glucose, which is the primary food for many organisms, which in turn are eaten by others, and so it goes on. There are countless series of plants and animals which depend on one another for existence. Such series are called *food chains* because each link invariably exists because of the one before it, and for the sake of the one that follows. In the sea, the rule is that the most minute plant-life called phytoplankton, is the beginning of everything. They provide food for small crabs or snails, which are eaten by the smaller fishes, which are again preyed upon by the larger fishes and so on. And these food chains can be seriously affected by pesticides.

Certain toxins cannot be broken down any further, whether they are in a spray, on a plant or in a fatty tissue. These substances remain poisonous, although their virulence decreases as years go by. It takes at least thirty–fifty years for the harmful effects of DDT and similar compounds to wear off.

Because plants and animals absorb these poisons from their food, this means that the amount of poison at every following level in the food chain becomes correspondingly greater as it accumulates, until, in the end it reaches an animal which consumes so much poison that it dies. These are usually the 'higher' species of animals, at the top of a food chain. Sandwich terns, hawks, sea eagles and even penguins are known to have been killed off by poisons used on agricultural pesticides. These poisons are carried to the sea in ground water, streams and rivers. Or they turn up in small mammals

which have eaten treated plants or seeds, and the mammals
fall prey to the hawks, cats and other species.

Eider ducks

The fate of the eider duck is a case in point. Eiders are skilful
divers, living on fish and molluscs. They are the suppliers of
the famous eiderdown. The females pluck the down from
their breasts and bodies to make a warm lining for their nests.
On Terschelling eiderdown collecting used to be very profitable, and the collectors knew exactly how much they could
take from the nests. The female only has enough down on her
body for a nest and a half. So the collectors took only a small
quantity from each nest before the breeding season and
waited until the fledgling had left before taking the rest. To
keep this trade in down flourishing, it was regarded as a crime
to kill the eider duck, steal eggs or gather too much down. But
nowadays, the eider duck is very rarely found on
Terschelling. More than ten thousand eider ducks existed on
the Wadden (or Friesian) Islands, off the coasts of the
Netherlands and Germany, until 1962. After that, the eggs
began breaking in the nests, broody females died, and after
1966 not a single egg hatched out. The reason? The waters of
the Rhine and Maas contain large quantities of Dieldrin and
Telodrin, substances with many characteristics similar to
those of DDT. They first found their way into the smallest
water organisms, then into the fishes, and finally into the fat of
the eider duck. While the female is brooding, she does not
consume any food but lives on her fat. It has been found that
by the end of the breeding season the female eider can
have absorbed seventeen times as much insecticide into her
bloodstream as at the beginning – and this concentration is
fatal. The breaking of eggshells is also attributable to the
insecticides, because the calcium content of the shell is
weakened by the increased concentration of the poisons. The
cause of the serious intestinal parasitic infection in dead and
dying eider ducks is probably due to the fact that the birds

have been weakened by the toxins, giving the parasites their opportunity. Gradually now the eider population is building up again, because the use of this type of pesticide is slowly meeting opposition in north-west Europe.

Dolphins

Dolphins used to be very popular visitors to the shores of 'our' island. Playing and leaping they ventured close to the beach. They were entertaining creatures, intelligent and mysterious visitors from what is called the 'fourth world'. But those days are gone too, and dolphins are hardly ever sighted here now, or if they are, are slaughtered. This happened recently, when a young dolphin chanced to swim into the island's harbour, as in days gone by. The triangular fin which sheared through the water made people panic. A shark! It was clubbed to death. Soon afterwards, the mother dolphin swam into the harbour in search of her young. She was not clubbed to death however. She was ill and swam to her death against the basalt blocks of the harbour.

The dolphins, porpoises and whales belong to *one* family, of which eighty species are known. They are the most highly developed creatures in the sea, but very little is known about them. Of all animals in the world, the development of their brains most closely resembles that of man's. They are mammals, which have to come to the surface in order to breathe. Some of them have to surface once or twice a minute, but others can remain under water for as long as two hours. Until a few years ago there were half a million dolphins killed each year, largely in the course of tuna fisheries in the eastern Pacific ocean. In taking the tuna, so popular in 'Salade Niçoise' and in pet foods, one of the main species sought is the yellowfin tuna. For reasons unknown, the yellowfin generally swim below schools of dolphins. This makes the catching easy. Boats round up the dolphins into enormous purse-nets and the tuna follow. But the dolphins get caught in the nets and drown, and their families stay near them and eventually drown too, or get hauled onto the ship, then flung back into the water, often dying of shock or injury. In America new regulations have improved matters and their boats killed about 26,000 dolphins in 1977, and new catching methods are helping. But now the boats of other nations are increasing their catch of tuna – and thus, in many cases, of dolphins.

Yet the dolphin has been a good friend of man since ancient times. The many seamen's tales about drowning men who have been helped by dolphins probably have a grain of truth in them. When a dolphin is unwell and has difficulty in coming up to breathe, the others come to his assistance and nudge him upwards. Then why shouldn't dolphins ever have performed the same service for a drowning human being?

Whales

The number of whales is decreasing rapidly. One species after another is becoming endangered as a result of excessive hunting. In the past, whenever the supply seems to have been exhausted, new techniques came to the assistance of the whalers – faster ships, sonar, and so on. The first to be caught were the slow-moving species, which could be approached with rowing boats. These whales have the fortunate habit of sinking straight down when harpooned and then re-emerging in the same place. So it was easy to butcher them. As early as the eleventh century, Basques started to hunt the black right whales in the Bay of Biscay. This species was commonly found in large numbers in temperate zones. Ten thousand were caught every year off New Zealand alone until a short time ago. Now they are nearly extinct.

The Greenland right whale met the same fate. The hunt for this species was a great source of prosperity in the seven-teenth and eighteenth centuries. Grey, weathered stakes stand scattered about on 'our' island, hidden between clumps of alders. They are pieces from the jawbones of whales, souvenirs of the years when whalehunters left this island for Greenland looking for their fortune. There are two sleepy old towns in the polders north of Amsterdam, Graft and De Rijp, whose splendid town halls bear witness to the former riches. Long ago, when these places still had access to the sea, they were flourishing centres of the whaling industry. North American whaling, too, covered the entire northern Atlantic. Sometimes the ships stayed away for years, in order to return laden with oil for lamps and train oil and baleen for umbrellas and corsets. Masters and shipowners from old whaling centres such as New Bedford and Stonington grew rich from this, as we can still see today from their splendid houses. The Greenland right whale became commercially extinct just after the turn of the century – there were so few it was no longer profitable to go after them. So now they are taken on a very small scale by Eskimos. Even so, this may lead to their extinction. For they are probably the most endangered of all whale species.

Another of the baleen whales – those which live off planktonic crustacea (krill) and tiny fish which they strain from the water – is the humpback whale. It is a squat animal, weighing up to 45,000 kilos, although it is only seventeen metres long. It is well known for its remarkable songs which have even been made into commercial discs. The humpback whale is also known for its ability to leap high out of the water and turn a backward somersault.

When the slow-moving species ceased to be profitable, then it was the turn of the swift species, many of which are very large.

The world record for deep sea diving by mammals is indisputably held by the sperm whale. This enormous animal can probably go down as far as 7,000 feet. A drowned sperm whale was once found at a depth of 3,720 feet, entangled in a telephone cable. The sperm whale hunts for squid in the obscurity of these great depths. Because it is a mammal it cannot extract any oxygen from the water, for it has no gills, but the fact that it can hunt for fishes which have gills at such a depth proves that oxygen is still present there. Its presence is possible because vertical streams exchange the water from the depths with oxygen-rich water of the surface (a warning for those who think that waste from nuclear power stations can be dumped on the sea bed without any danger). It has been estimated that the number of sperm whales has declined from a million to nearly half that number. Every year, about 15–20,000 sperm whales are killed for their sperm oil, from the great head and the blubber. It has unique properties and is in great demand, mainly for softening fashion leathers and in lubricating oil for precision machinery. For this reason, although it was 'immortalized' by Herman Melville in his book *Moby Dick*, the sperm whale will probably not continue to exist for very long, if we do not succeed in limiting the catch quotas.

But we shall not achieve this simply by pointing out its useful qualities. The demand for the limited supply of sperm oil is too great an incentive for maintaining high quotas. Some nature conservationists have been alive to this, and the formation of 'Endangered Species Productions' is an attempt to save the whale from destruction by developing a substitute product. Learning from the struggle against more and more aggressive whaling, some nature conservationists are now turning directly to the users of whale oil, to offer them alternatives. The whale oil most in demand is sperm oil, which appears to be practically identical to that from jojoba seed. The jojoba plant is a wild shrub which grows in the American desert. Although it has not been possible to cultivate the plant so far, and the harvest therefore still has to be obtained from the wild plants, it is expected that it will be possible to make jojoba plantations in the poor, arid desert regions of the Sahel countries and the bare Indian reservations of North America in time to come. And now Third World countries may be expected to support the anti-whaling actions, which they used to regard merely as a hobby of the rich countries. But there are many substitutes which already exist, and so, by offering the processors competitive products it will be possible to make whaling less remunerative, according to the new-style conservationists. Some of the action-groups, such as the Greenpeace Organisation, have gone over to drastic counter-actions and have made use of a

couple of ships, including a former Canadian minesweeper,
with volunteers to obstruct the hunters in the course of
whaling.

The blue whale is the largest animal that has ever lived on
earth. This leviathan is four times as large as the prehistoric
brontosaurus which people gape at in museums. It grows to a
length of more than thirty metres and weighs a hundred and
fifty tons.

We should stop and ask ourselves why this wonder of the
world should have to die. Can anyone think of one good
reason? Why does the world spend millions to preserve the
temples of Angkor, Borobudur or Abu Simbel? Is it because
they are large and important; or because they have been the
work of generations? Estimates indicate that about two
hundred thousand specimens of the blue whale used to exist:
now there are only five or six per cent remaining. The chance
of survival is very small. In less than forty years, mankind
practically managed to destroy the inheritance of 27 million
years. They are tracked down by radar and helicopters. They
are chased by fast-moving boats. They are killed with
explosive harpoons fired from cannons. And there is a floating
factory to render them down into oil and other products. Cat
and dog food, for example – in 'bite-sized chunks' no doubt.
And cosmetics. That the greatest creature ever to have lived
ends up as night cream. Truly, our culture must have reached
its peak! In the mid 1960s the major whaling nations, too late
as usual, agreed to stop hunting the blue whale. Now they
continue catching the fin whale, sei, bryde's, minke and
sperm. There are some fifteen nations which continue whaling. But Japan and Russia, between them, take nearly 80% of
the total catch. Both are members of the International
Whaling Commission which is responsible for limiting the
numbers caught. In spite of this, too many whales are caught
and those with a vested commercial interest carry
on, in a frantic race to catch whatever there is left to
catch.

Greed, rivalry and the inability to reach an agreement are
the reasons why the oceans of the world are being depleted.

And all this is rooted in the old practice of everyone spending nature's capital.

What capital do we mean? In 1967–68, 44,645 whales were killed. At that time, fourteen floating factories were still in action, which made use of 210 fast catchers. 212,000 tons of whale and sperm oil were produced and 56,000 tons of meal, livermeal and so-called 'so lubles'. In the year 1961–62, the number of animals killed had been 66,090, while the yield in oil and meal was roughly twice that above. In these years, the value of all the products mentioned above has dropped from £38 million to £13.6 million. It is clear that an extensive branch of industry is on the verge of bringing about its own downfall. If a larger stock of whales could be maintained, the world would have an enormous source of fats and proteins at its disposal, and a *permanent* source! For then we should only use the surplus, the annual excess, the interest. Mother nature would continue to produce the 'raw materials' for a vast food industry and there would be no expenses for investment, upkeep or wages.

The minute plant life in the ocean is eaten by tiny creatures (zooplankton). All the great whales (except for the squid-eating sperm whale) live on these tiny creatures and convert them into flesh and fat. It is a very short food chain and completely impossible for man to imitate, but with proper planning we can profit from this natural supply for centuries to come. (However, one essential condition for this is that more humane methods of capture would have to be developed.) But all commercial whaling must be banned for at least ten years to allow the whale population to start building up again.

Apart from the hypothetical possibility of a continuous supply of food, other values should not be overlooked. A million-dollar recreation industry has grown up because of the intelligence of these marine mammals. Films and television have a growing tendency to use them as unpaid actors. Dolphins, and also the killer-whale (or orca), are used in all kinds of ways, as 'watchdogs', 'trackers', 'messengers' and 'carriers'. There has been much research on how they can help in military operations but not a great deal on what good they can do for man. The great cetaceans have been an almost unstudied group for a very long time. Like other animals, they developed from primitive life-forms in the sea about 500 million years ago. They became land animals at one period in their evolution: later they returned to the water. This is why they are still mammals and take oxygen from the air with lungs, not out of the water with gills.

Dolphins and other species of whales possess sensory powers from which man, with all his technique, has a great deal to learn. They can 'see' without using their eyes, with the aid of a system called '*sonar*'. Using sonar, the position of objects can be fixed by picking up reflections of sound waves. Blindfolded dolphins in shows retrieve objects for the amuse-ment of the public using sonar. Even stranger is the fact that dolphins and some other whale species can 'talk' to one another. But we still do not understand their communication system, although we know they use high-frequency vib-rations as a private language. In this way, a mother and her young can pin-point each other's position even though they may be miles apart. It seems that every individual has a signal (or 'name') of its own, with which it signs its messages. Sometimes, when danger threatens, the whole chorus sud-denly falls silent, apparently as a result of a warning signal being passed on.

In the Amazon and the Indus, there are freshwater dol-phins. The Indus dolphin is blind. Because the water in this river is turbid and murky this dolphin has lost the use of its eyes. With sonar, it can move about perfectly well. Research in this field may help in producing aids for blind people to find their way around more easily. 'Natura artis magistra'; nature is the teacher of all things and not of art alone!

The significance of the dolphin for man is that it represents just *one* of the many examples from nature to which science and technology owe a great deal and from which they still have a great deal to learn. The 'capital' value of nature, as a source for scientific investigation and technical invention based on it, is immeasurably large. Some economists may feel a need to estimate this value: but economists also use the concept 'infinite' for something which is of exceptionally great importance. The dolphin should be considered this way. It is not only an outstanding subject for scientific research but has also a very strong appeal, because the dolphin is to the sea what man is to the land: the most highly-developed mammal.

Some biologists and nature conservationists object to an argument which uses the value of industrial oil or fat production from whales and dolphins, or their value to science as reasons for preserving them. They abhor these examples because they reduce these intelligent animals to the level of utility objects.

This view is easy to understand, but there is another aspect. Though the biologist and the nature conservationist may regard it as a remarkable animal, using another, economic, set of standards it is merely a utility object. The assessment of these animals for their usefulness and profitability can be regarded as *supplementary*. The animal is none the worse off if it can also fit into the values of people who care nothing for nature conservation. Unfortunately, it is not enough for the conservationist to take the moral or ethical viewpoint. The attitude is very noble but has not proved to be very useful. It is no use pleading the aesthetic value of nature (or of whales in this case) to the commercially minded economist. For him we must produce commercial and economic arguments.

Vanishing habitats

Animals are not only exterminated because man hunts them down until the very last specimen has been wiped out. A much commoner reason is that the conditions for life disappear.

Every living creature needs a certain 'habitat'. A complex of conditions in space and time which is essential for the species, and through which feeding, living and reproducing become possible. If that habitat is disturbed or destroyed,

then the species is doomed to destruction. The most important living environments for species of plants and animals are
the oceans of the world and the tropical rain forests. The
rapidly spreading process of over-fishing and marine pollution is comparatively recent. The attack on the forests is,
however, almost as old as humankind itself, and the consequences can be seen only too plainly. Ten thousand years
ago the Sahara was a subtropical paradise. It became a desert
as a result of erosion and subsequent loss of fertile soil. From
the vast forests of the Lebanon, of which the Bible speaks,
only a few remnants are left. The woodlands of ancient
Greece, of Italy in the time of the Romans and of mediaeval
Spain are all gone. All this has happened through felling trees
for temples, shipbuilding and houses, through inefficient
methods of agriculture, because of erosion and, particularly,
because of goats. The goats of the Mediterranean countries
devoured the last green remains of the landscape. Every shoot
that tried to grow into a tree or bush was bitten off before it
had a chance.

Another disaster is the deliberate destruction of nature on
the largest scale ever, which took place in Vietnam in the
'sixties, but will probably yet be surpassed by what is going to
happen in the Amazon area.

In December 1974, Joao Delgas Frisch, vice-president of
the Brazilian association for nature conservation stated: 'The
Amazon region will be a desert in ten years' time. A rain of
arsenic, a rain of death, is falling over this green part of the
world'. Since 1970, the Amazon jungle has been sprayed day
in, day out with the defoliants which Brazil has bought from
America at a bargain price after the latter had withdrawn
from Vietnam. Some of the herbicides kill plants by interfer-
ing with their photosynthesis and so stopping the growth. But
others stimulate growth with hormones, so that the plant or
tree quickly outgrows its strength, and dies. In the name of
'progress', the forests of the Amazon are being wiped off the
face of the earth by giant bulldozers which advance in rows,
linked together by chains with great iron balls attached. But
the soil of the tropical jungle cannot stand exposure to the

sun. The layer of humus is only a few centimetres thick, for the plants rot away very quickly because of the great heat and humidity, and the nutrients are immediately taken in by the growing plants. In a healthy forest the sun cannot penetrate to this thin layer of humus, but when defoliation and deforestation allow it to shine directly onto the earth, the humus layer disappears and the ground changes into laterite, an infertile kind of clay. The humus is washed away by the tropical downpours, and the herbicides with it. They will kill the plankton in the rivers, so that the fish and other animals living on them will also be killed. When natural cover disappears and erosion takes hold in an area like this, it turns into a bare, brown desert, where the rich plant and animal life stand no chance of survival. It is an ecological catastrophe on a world scale, causing tens of thousands of higher plant and animal species and countless lower species to be lost for ever. And apart from all this, the climate in South America, and possibly all over the world, will be changed drastically.

Why do such disasters happen? Brazil and many other countries have acquired a taste for 'economic growth'. They are poor communities wanting to develop into modern societies. Roads and cities have to come, surrounded by agricultural and cattle-raising areas, although in most places the soil is not at all suitable. People want to be modern, grow and prosper. Western technology and western economy are used as a model for this growth, even though they are probably bad examples for non-western countries. But it is still not too late. These countries still have a chance to avoid following the poor examples of America and Europe. They are still not too far progressed to improve matters by adopting a system of 'economic growth' which leaves the natural conditions for survival intact: something which has never been achieved before.

The Spanish economy, under Philip II in the 16th century, is a case in point. Spain then experienced unprecedented growth: shipyards flourished thanks to the building of countless men-of-war. Sea battles were fought against the Turks, against England and against the rebellious Low

Countries, which ended only in the downfall of the invincible Armada, the greatest fleet of all times, in the Channel and North Sea. These wars were possible thanks to the gold and silver which were found in South America, and because the capital of nature was eaten into. Every year, thousands of hectares of centuries-old forests were felled in order to build the enormous fleet and keep it in good repair. But already, by the end of the seventeenth century, great famines afflicted the Iberian peninsula, which saw its glory and riches disappear with its forests and fertile soils.

In the place where vast forests of oaks had once stood, erosion gained ground rapidly, and only bare rocks were left. Nature and living environment, animals and plants, water and soil, all fall victim to a short-term exploitation which is – quite mistakenly – called 'economic growth'.

Four. The Pursuit of Prosperity

> 'Nature conservation has become an interdisciplinary occupation to an increasing degree. First there were mainly biologists. Then, ecologists also began to play a part as well as the ethologists, who study animal behaviour. Recently, economists also appear to have become of great importance.'
> Prince Bernhard

Economic Growth

What then is 'economic growth'? Firstly, it is *not* a law of nature, which people *must* obey. It is a fabrication, a supposition, a policy, a process which people need in their attempts to make their existence richer, more enjoyable and more prosperous. It is having *more* to share, a *greater* chance of survival, *more* ways of escaping the harshness of the environment, which set its natural forces loose on our ancestors. For them there were inescapable catastrophes, so that hunger, sickness and death were regular guests of the family. Economic growth was a necessity but it is becoming more and more plain now, that this 'growth' is sapping the foundations on which it was built. Economic growth is a process intended to lighten our existence but which has the opposite effect. So there is something wrong with it.

How has it happened that a system of economic planning was adopted which brings about an increasing measure of confusion? How can society go on developing in the same way without, at the same time, making the mistake of undermining its own existence? And, if nature really is so valuable, and if economics has to take this into account, then what is the exact value of nature? Of course, this economic growth had its reasons, a number of which have been put forward for conquering nature, for mastering it and destroying it to serve the growth. So what are the reasons?

Science and technology have spent centuries searching for methods of improving the human lot. Ignorant beings, living in fear at the bottom of a mysterious universe and trembling before the fate that can strike every day, stand a great chance that fate will, indeed, be cruel. Prosperous twentieth century citizens of western countries can scarcely visualize the conditions in which their ancestors lived for tens of centuries. Yet, only twenty five years ago most houses were without central heating. The simple stoves were cold every morning and full of acrid ashes; there was no hot water on tap, and electricity was too expensive for even the simplest appliance to be used. And we only have to look back half a century to find the last remains of the wretched conditions in which the inhabitants of the cold North, too, had to live.

Now, most prosperous citizens think that poverty is something that only belongs to the Third World. Most young people do not have the faintest idea how recent and exceptional is the luxury in which they are living. Heroism, prosperity, art and romanticism are almost all that stand out from the past. The seventeenth century was a Dutch century of riches and glory; the eighteenth French; and the nineteenth, English. Spain and Portugal flourished in the fifteenth and sixteenth centuries. And the Italian renaissance had already started in the thirteenth century. So every part of Europe experienced a period of cultural peak, of unprecedented prosperity and, later, of decline. But the glory is the picture that now penetrates to the consciousness, and it determines our conception of history. The masterpieces which fill our museums dazzle us by their beauty, technique, piety and composition. Splendid palaces and castles bear witness to an equally dazzling art and culture. In other words, the high peaks of culture are all we see of the past – not the misery. And this is self-evident. The commonplace wretchedness consisted of hovels and hungry paupers, who were forgotten or only painted by a few, such as El Greco, Jeroen Bosch or Jan Steen. Very few look any further than the shining varnish of cultural history, but for centuries the great

majority were poor or suffering. A passionate longing for
development and improvement of the well-being of mankind
and, indeed, for *economic growth*, came into existence. The
position in which people now earning minimum wages find
themselves would have been one of unimaginable luxury to
the paupers living then. Warmth, food, clothing and housing
are no longer such problems as they were.

The phase theory

In social history there is a widely accepted division into three
parts – the so-called phase theory. Understanding this might
help us to understand the process of 'economic growth'.
Mankind went through three phases of development; the
biological the social and the individual phases.

In the *biological* phase, man lives like an animal. He fights
for survival and struggles to keep himself and his family alive.
He lives in comparative poverty, as a primitive hunter and
food-gatherer and cannot permit himself to worry about the
future, but lives from day to day. Only in a few instances does
a tribe or family succeed in living in any sort of harmony with
surrounding nature, because their particular circumstances
are favourable. But this is rare. The concept of 'The Noble
Savage', the harmonious natural man dating from the
Romantic era, is an idealistic notion of existence in this
primitive biological phase. The concept is false. Most of
humanity is a helpless victim in this phase and not a partner of
nature.

If there is a drought, there is hunger. If it is cold, it has to be
endured. Sickness usually means death. If there is no game,
there is no food. No thought is given to tomorrow, so this is
uncertain. Only 'today' counts; evening is still far-off and
perhaps nothing will be caught today, which means hunger.
And one could not afford to experiment, for this would bring
still more uncertainties. Obedience to tradition, and hier-
archy, are therefore essential. Only the group is important,
the individual has no significance. Certainly, some primitive

races here and there in the world still live in harmony with their surroundings, but they are the exceptions, not the rule. With the great majority of, what people are accustomed to calling, 'primitive tribes' sickness and hunger are more normal phenomena than health and prosperity.

The *social phase* is the next step. People are a little more astute than the animals around them. They are beginning to understand the forces of nature, to which they felt subjected at first, and are starting to turn them to their own use. Huts are built and clothes made. Religious rituals come into existence for the appeasement of gods and spirits who would otherwise let things go badly for the group. House and ritual have similar functions: one affords protection against cold and rain, and the other against the powers which bring the cold and rain. Agriculture is a breakthrough in this phase. Anyone practising agriculture also has to think about the day after tomorrow. He has to know the seasons, and when to sow and harvest. He has to start thinking about *organisation*. Organised agriculture is a gigantic step, only equalled in history by the industrial revolution. Compared with the practices of the nomads who wandered with their cattle from one grazing ground to another, and the primitive hunters and food gatherers who had no idea of organisation or the laws of nature, planned agriculture has been a significant advance – one which, indeed, has yet to take place in some parts of the world. Even in many agricultural areas, lack of understanding and over-cropping still prevail.

Planned agriculture involves thinking about such subjects as: how much land do I have to prepare; which seeds should I sow and when; what will the harvest yield; and, do I have the right implements? These questions are technical ones to start with but the farmer has to understand the technical basis of agriculture. However, there is a second important aspect. Because the number of hours a farmer can work is limited, because his piece of ground is not infinitely great and because he can grow different crops, he has to choose what he will do. This choice between different possibilities and limitations is something that had never happened before.

So choice is a milestone which leads to a refinement and intensification of agriculture. This leads to the creation of *food surpluses*, which has far-reaching consequences because trade and industry proceed from this. When more food becomes available than the farmers need for themselves, two things happen. Firstly, they can try to barter their surplus for goods which they cannot make themselves. In addition, the creation of this surplus means that some people do not have to occupy themselves with food production any longer. They can concentrate on producing goods which the farmers would like to have but cannot make, or on fetching those desired articles from distant places. Craftsmen, merchants and transporters, markets, trade routes and an increasingly complicated system of agreements and rules come into existence, to make all this run smoothly. All kinds of organisations grow up, with whose help social security is increased: guilds and orders, trading companies and navies, commercial treaties and political agreements.

In the social phase, there is an even greater contrast between animal, man and his primitive ancestors. Whereas the animal becomes adapted to the natural environment, man subordinates his surroundings to himself with increasing ingenuity and increasing success. Technology, trade, production and health services stand shoulder to shoulder in the fight against the environment which is beaten to its knees in no more than a few centuries with twentieth century industrial man as the final victor. At least, so it appears to him.

When people know how to organise their dealings with the environment better, they become better off. This means in practice, the more efficiently they can control their surroundings, the more benefit they will derive from them. So *misuse* of the surroundings (nature and environment) is out-of-place in a well-organised economy. For, anyone who understands his (natural) environment well, will know better than to inflict so much harm on it that he will himself be injured by the damage.

The science of economics translated this organization of the environment into '*production-factors*': *land, capital and labour* and the better these are correlated, the better will be the result. When the production factors utilized are balanced, a greater return is recorded. Supported by the development of agriculture, science and technology, the production factors are the flywheel of the industrial revolution. Revolution means complete change. Industrial production is a real change in the course of history for, thanks to this revolution, man would be 'set free': he would be able to escape from his natural fate for ever. No longer was the goal simply to survive, but to become free; blessed with the products of technology and industry.

Once he was free, he would finally enter the third phase, the *individual phase*. Here, man is free to give full scope to his natural talents; he makes free choices, is not a slave of production, nor subject to nature, but is highly developed. He is in a position to be the enjoyer of culture, which he really ought to be, as the crown on creation.

The *Gross National Product* (GNP) came into existence as a statistical means of measuring whether this economic growth really had been achieved. It is calculated by simply adding up the product of all existing industry. The more production there is, the greater is the combined income and, therefore, *prosperity*; this was the line of thought. So increased production became the yardstick for the GNP. And a simple way of reasoning arose, which still dominates modern society: that is, an increase in the GNP means economic growth, thus an increase in income, thus an increase in prosperity. This is good for us. So production has to be encouraged wherever possible. The most important incentive to production is the remuneration of the producer, which is called profit. Production is good for the community, profit is good for the producer. And the one who makes a great deal of profit accordingly is a social *success*. He is *'getting on in the world'*.

So production became holy and the production system became an end that justified a number of its means. These included (and sometimes still do): the exploitation of children, the grinding-down of workers, oppression of other peoples, use of their resources, stench, noise, long working

days, low wages and *misuse and over-exploitation of nature.*
Production became a snake biting its own tail. The means
became more and more the end: production for the sake of
production and no longer for the sake of 'liberation', the
change over to the third, individual, phase.

It has taken about a hundred years of social development to
improve the conditions of workers. Through a ban on child
labour, social legislation and ever-improving safety measures
for workers, conditions have now been attained which can be
seen to be distinct corrections to the, formerly, unchallenge-
able, freedom of the producer. This process, of making ever
further-reaching corrections, is still going on. Products have
to meet all kinds of health and safety requirements. Working
conditions will have to become healthier and safer and
employees are gradually coming to have a greater say in the
labour process.

If an end is put to the most persistent form of over-
exploitation – *that of nature and its resources* – then the third
phase, the full development of a liberated human being, will
be closer for people from all social classes. If it is not achieved,
then a return to pre-industrial revolution living conditions
will be likely. Soil erosion, exhaustion of mineral wealth,
water and air pollution, loss of a large variety of species and of
natural living conditions will all lead to a situation in which
nature, crippled, will hit back hard. And yet we go on with the
subjugation of nature, with 'progress for the general good and
to the greater glory of . . .' Yes, of what or who, exactly?

In most western countries, health problems and social
insecurity have been largely eliminated. In spite of this, we
want to keep on 'growing', although the sense of doing so has
practically disappeared. Yet, this growth is not without its
dangers. Some try to explain this insistence, on going on with
an activity which no longer has any meaning, from the point
of view of the so-called ethos of change or belief in progress.
They postulate that it arises from the awareness of one's own
imperfection and the actual impossibility of living up to the
Christian ideal. Man himself has to take the blame for the
imperfection of his state, and so must do penance: discharge

his duties and labour 'in the sweat of his brow', even though the result of this labour is no longer the subjugation or adaptation of a cruel nature, but its destruction, which will finally affect him as well. Trimbos writes, 'Above all, in the early years of Christianity, with its expectation that the end of the world was at hand, preoccupation with the hereafter was a characteristic feature'. 'This attitude lost its religious roots much later. It made way for the optimism and positivism of nineteenth century thinking. Theology and a belief in providence have been superseded by an equal belief in science and technology. And therefore we use science and technology to obtain an increase in production, supposing that this will not only lead to new prosperity but even to a kind of earthly deliverance from all the evil in ourselves and others'.

So man changes the environment, an activity which he generally calls 'progress'. The conviction that this change will always bring about an improvement prevents him from turning back even when he sees that the result of his efforts appears to be greater chaos: not only a seriously polluted environment, but also the signs that hunger, shortages of some raw materials and exhaustion of others are taking catastrophic shape. Inspired, but limited by the behaviour of the last two hundred years, his response to these signals is to *intensify* this behaviour and increase production; more technology, more exploitation. In the nineteen twenties, Herbert Hoover, President of the United States, said that, with God's help, the moment would soon come when poverty would be driven from the land. In 1930, John Maynard Keynes predicted, in his famous essay '*Economic Possibilities for our Grandchildren*', that prosperity and plenty would be available to everyone before the end of the century. In the 'fifties and 'sixties, western industrial countries experienced an unprecedented growth of production. This led to an abundance of material goods such as had never been seen before, giving rise to great optimism and a genuine belief in the sound judgement of the great Keynes.

Marx, too, forecast the paradise which would come when the great struggle had been fought: 'A world in which nobody has any narrowly-circumscribed occupation, but can train for any employment he chooses: thanks to socialized production the community makes it possible for me to do this today and that tomorrow, to go hunting in the morning and fishing in the afternoon, to breed cattle, and to grumble about the food in the evening – all just as it suits me, without becoming a hunter, a fisherman, a cattle breeder or a critic'.

If, according to Marx, this prosperity would come about as a result of winning the class-struggle, others thought that material wealth would only really be possible through the theory and practice of what, in the 'sixties, began to be called 'the New Economy'.

According to the New Economy, it ought to be possible for the existing economic growth to be maintained for decades to come, perhaps even a hundred years. If the tempo stayed high enough, a lasting victory over depression and recession ought to be gained and a permanent, and increasing flow of material goods would be guaranteed. How great this belief was has been expressed in very emphatic terms by Walter Heller, former Chairman of the Council of Economic Advisers to Presidents Kennedy and Johnson. 'The New Economy does not distinguish itself because it is new, but rather because it has brought home to management the lessons of modern economy – of Keynes and the Classics.' And the consequence of this has been, according to Heller, 'that economics has become adult at last, and that this once so disputed science has now become a lively political art'. According to him, modern economy has infiltrated into every corner of political and business undertakings, so making them great. He said, 'The significance of the great expansion in the 'sixties is not solely to be found in fine statistical data about (full) employment, income and growth, but above all in the shining promise of things which are to come'.

Barely a decade later this promise has faded; unemployment is increasing, growth has come to a standstill, the world is in the grip of inflation and the gloomiest forecasts are being made with increasing regularity. The former Chairman of the Canadian Economic Council, the well-known economist

John Deutsch, says, 'The desperate plight of mankind is this: there are no universally applicable solutions, no promising new doctrines, only difficult and disagreeable choices. The magic solutions of Keynes are exhausted'.

Why does production become a snake biting its own tail? What has gone wrong with human thought and action, with all its diligent and efficient organisation? This is what Erich Fromm writes about it: 'Modern industrial man works, fights and toils on, but is vaguely conscious of a feeling that there is no point in all his activities. While his power over material things is growing and he is continually creating newer and better means of commanding nature, he feels at the same time that he is enmeshed in a network of these selfsame means. He has lost sight of the only thing which is able to give real significance to these means, seeing that he is the reason for them and their final goal: man himself. While making himself the ruler of nature on the one hand, on the other he became the slave of the machine which he made with his own hands'.

The dream is over. The drive towards eternally increasing production leads into a blind alley. Evidently, the limits of growth have been reached and are even worked out by a computer. The utterances of the Club of Rome are only the first from a swelling chorus of prophets of doom and pessimism. All of them see the limits of human activities looming up in those very places where they once thought to conquer the vast riches of the earth and enjoy them.

The famous economist Robert Heilbroner commented: 'We shall try to rationalize it, we shall try to put the figures as honestly and as favourably as possible, but we cannot avoid admitting that we are unable to satisfy the demands of an increased growth of industrialization in this world when we take existing resources and the capacity of the fragile biosphere into account.' 'Then is there still hope for mankind?' 'If we ask ourselves whether it is possible to alleviate the needs of the future without having to pay a terrible price, then the answer is: No, there is no hope'. Indeed the behaviour of economists, entrepreneurs and politicians does not make one feel very hopeful, especially when, in hard times, they fall

back on means which they expect will lead to *more* production; but this only results in *further* technological violence
and *further* exhaustion of natural resources. For, anyone who
thinks about this must be aware that the increasingly detrimental effects of production cannot be solved by what caused
them. Economic thinking and acting have to be re-aligned
with the original aim: to strive for prosperity and be better off
in the widest possible sense.

This evokes the question: what is prosperity? *According to
existing economic views*, does modern planned economy lead to
the reverse of prosperity? And do the present inflation,
unemployment, exhaustion of raw materials and large-scale
destruction of nature have anything to do with one another?
The capital, technique and ingenuity which was used to attain
the present prosperity was accumulated over thousands of
years. In order to keep pace with the increase in world
population, and to satisfy its material needs, production has
to be doubled in less than twenty five years. If this can ever be
achieved, using the same means as now, then the price will be
incredibly high. Not only will the earth's crust be plundered
but we will have an overburdened and probably fatally
injured biosphere – the natural living environment, which is
the *source* of the prosperity we are seeking. This is the *natural
capital*, which ought to have its continuous existence guaranteed. Broadly speaking, this capital supplies all the conditions
necessary for human existence on earth. This means it covers
everything that is on or in the earth and the surrounding
atmosphere. In the past, economic science has given very
little attention to nature as a *capital property*. This is under-
standable for, as a branch of science, economics limits itself to
the question of choice in the use of means, each of which can
be used in a variety of ways. As far as natural capital is
concerned, until relatively recently only land was looked on as
economic property. It never occurred to anyone that the rest
of nature could be in short supply. There was plenty of fresh
air and clean water. There was a bountiful supply of trees for
felling in the woods, and the woodlands had, at most, some
value as a reservoir for future timber and firewood and would

also hold some game.

As Kenneth Boulding says, this was the time of the *cowboy economy*. There are always new horizons and unknown areas with undiscovered treasures, but attention to one's own living environment is a chance occurrence. Anything in man's way has to give ground so when it becomes too oppressive in the cities, people who can afford it take refuge in the countryside. Obviously, this treatment of nature can only last as long as the bearing capacity of the nature remaining can stand it. Human interference can finally go to such extremes that nature is past recovery. Now that people are at last coming to understand that pressure on the environment has increased in an unacceptable way, the science of economics, too, is beginning to pay more attention to the significance of the natural capital.

The theory of 'cowboy economy' has now been succeeded by the '*spaceship* theory'. The world is a spaceship in which there is only a limited supply of everything. By human standards, only the energy which reaches the earth from the sun is inexhaustible. There is an important conclusion: when people use more of earth's supplies in a certain period than can be replenished in that same period with the help of the sun's energy, then we are eating into our natural capital.

The photographs taken of the earth from space strengthen this image of 'spaceship earth'. (It is a striking coincidence that these photographs were taken at the same time at which the report of the Club of Rome appeared.) In the heyday of technical achievement, many people suddenly became aware of the limitations of the globe. At the very moment when technical ingenuity seemed to show that there were no limits to the distances and explorations mankind could solve, it became suddenly clear that the store cupboards of our earth are rapidly becoming bare.

It is important to look at this connection, between *more* production and *more* consumption on the one hand and the encroachment on the natural capital on the other, as an economic problem. For example, it is fairly generally accepted that if, at a certain moment, we want to ascertain whether a social system (a country's economy), is on the upgrade, we

compare the value of the national product for that year with
that of the previous year. If the first is greater than the second,
then we talk about growth and so of 'improvement'. Most
people find that a stock-breeder who has sold more produce
this year than last is prospering, but if his turnover has
increased because he has sold a part of his herd as well as his
milk, then he has encroached on his capital. In fact, something like this is always going on when analyzing economic
growth, but corrections for encroaching on available means of
production and supplies are lacking.

What is the significance of this for current opinions about
growth? We will deal first with the question of how far the
growth of production in past years has been caused by the
encroachment on natural capital. This is not a matter which
should be left solely to economists, for economists are not
very brilliant at interpreting the ecological relationships and
values which are lost in the growth of production. It is
especially important to realise that 'more' does not necessarily mean 'better'. We should ask, at what expense was
'more' gained. The poor understanding of what is being
sacrificed for production arises partly because people often do
not know what need is being satisfied or because an incorrect
value has been placed on it.

As an economic question, the encroachment on the natural
capital is directly concerned with the way people produce and
consume and with their concept of prosperity. You only have
'welfare' if you fare 'well'. Nature is just as essential for this as
production, but is mostly ignored. There was a time when
anyone who liked to go walking or cycling in the wood close to
his home and wanted peace and quiet or to see a clear lake or a
beautiful stream had plenty of choice. In most cases, anyone
cherishing the same wish in 1978 will be disappointed
because few of these natural 'goods' are left. While people
imagine that they are becoming better off, these simple
wishes can no longer be fulfilled. In economic terms they are,
then, less prosperous. So human needs cannot be satisfied by
manufactured goods alone; human requirements are too
diverse. A part of our requirement is the production of

houses, furniture, cars, clothes, medicines and hospitals. But, if our organization were better, other requirements for manufactured produce ought *not* to exist. What is at stake here is not production but *protection* of the *things that were there already*: nature, with its earth, air, water, forests, fields, savannahs, jungles, heaths, rivers and lakes. Anyone who says that we do not need these natural things, in order to be 'prosperous', and that therefore economics might as well forget about nature, implies that people do not need to breathe, relax, indulge in leisure activities, become healthy or stay healthy; that people are not natural beings. There are many economists who imply this.

However, the Dutch economist Hueting takes the view that we need nature and that it is therefore important to our economy. He writes: '*When – from whatever motives – the general opinion prevails that our environment is in an unacceptable state and the government proceeds to take urgent steps with regard to production processes and habits of consumption, leading to a smaller quantity of goods and services being available, then the total satisfaction of needs obtained from economic goods is herewith increased. In this case, less production leads to greater prosperity*'. In other words, if it is generally recognized that nature and a healthy living environment are essential for prosperity, some incompatible industrial activities may be forbidden; less may be produced, but nature and the environment are better off and so prosperity is increased.

We have popularly defined prosperity as the state which has to be reached in order to exist or survive in a reasonable manner. Economists speak of prosperity if there is sufficient provision for our needs. A number of prerequisites for this will be appreciated through an understanding of human needs. The economists measure these needs by working with the concept of 'market', in which the demand for goods is answered by a supply. Among the goods people demand are *environmental goods*, none of which are, or are able to be, offered on the market – such as clean water, a wood or fresh air. Maslow, the psychologist, has listed the needs of every human being in order of priority, irrespective of where he

lives or to what culture he belongs. These are:
1 The need for food.
2 The need for protective shelter.
3 The need for protection of trunk and limbs (clothing, health).
4 The need for an identity of one's own.
5 The need to belong to others (a group, a tribe, a family).

Without exception, the goods which prosperous states produce for their 'economic subjects' (or consumers) can be classified in terms of how they satisfy the above-mentioned needs. For example, a car can satisfy the need for identity, for belonging to a group and for protective shelter. Similar consideration can be applied, in various ways, to such divergent goods as clothes, furniture, comestibles, books, holiday trips, tea sets or lampshades. There are countless ways, too, in which plants and animals can be used or have significance for man. Possibilities which are indeed used, consciously or unconsciously, because there is no way of living without them. Nobody can exist without clean water, fertile soil, clean air, or without trees and other greenery. We need all these to breathe, eat and produce. But they can only be recognised economically if we regard nature as *capital*. This expression brings out the resemblance between living nature and the concept of capital as used in economic planning. The latter includes for example, the assets (money) invested in shares, houses, factory buildings, machines, tools and a credit balance in the bank. The capital produces a yield and does not itself decline. The yield is called *interest* and is a part of the income, in addition to the income from work. Naturally people can use the income to buy the things they like to have. And the higher the income, the more ways there are to enjoy it.

However, income drops again if there is *less* interest so the aim is to keep the capital in first-class condition – thus to make buildings, houses and machines last as long as possible by maintaining them well. People do their utmost to obtain the highest possible yields with maximal efficiency. Shares are invested, the soil is tilled and fertilized, machines are lubricated, all so as to obtain the best possible result. What is taboo is encroaching on the capital itself. Everyone knows that there will not be any interest if the factory buildings sag and decay. A house where the rain and wind whistle through will not bring in any rent. Neither are shares sold if they still have to yield a dividend in successive years. The capital itself is unassailable. One leaves it alone.

If the capital in a business is encroached on, through a part of it being sold, the proceeds of the sale are not added up with the interest. It is not regarded as being part of the income, because it is loss of capital. All this is considered to be quite normal, because the continuity of the business (or the maintainance of its capital) is the most important thing. For if this capital should decline in value, the yield will decline too, and the continuity will be endangered. The strange thing is that, while this practice is quite a matter of course in business book-keeping, it is left out altogether in the book-keeping of a country.

This national book-keeping consists mainly of the calculation of the GNP. In the course of production, use is made of the natural (or social) capital (including water, earth, air and minerals). *But the natural capital is not respected, it is squandered.* So it would be appropriate to subtract a large sum from the national capital annually to compensate this loss. But the opposite is done. The faster this capital is depleted, the higher the GNP becomes and the more satisfied politicians, industrialists and economists become. The consumption of the natural capital is looked on as a good transaction.

What would happen if the theory and practice of business book-keeping were grafted on to the national book-keeping, so that nature, landscape and the raw materials consumed were taken into account? This is poorly considered in economic literature, an indication that most economists have little interest in the problem. For them, nature is still apparently something which does not count. But the few who do pay attention to it use various methods (of which more in later chapters). One example is called the compensation method:

A wood near a large town is visited by ten thousand people a day for their leisure. Apparently, the wood has a value for them which they gain by going for a walk in it. The wood satisfies a need and is *therefore of economic importance*. But the visitors do not pay an entrance fee and no great investments have been made in the wood. There are only a few maintenance costs which are paid by the government. Although this wood is used in various ways, for the sake of convenience we shall only consider its value from the point of view of recreation. The value of the wood for other purposes, such as hunting, scientific investigation, timber production, beautifying the landscape or purifying the air are disregarded for the time being.

How can the purely recreational value of the wood be assessed? Let us imagine for a moment that the wood was *not* there. There are ten thousand people who want to indulge in leisure activities. They need the wood. If it is not there, then another recreational area has to be provided in which these people can relax in a similar way. If the construction cost of this substitute (compensatory) area (for ten thousand visitors a day) is 12.5 million pounds for example, then the recreational value of the wood alone is at least £12.5 million.

The same argument would be valid for a river with clear water. Say a hundred thousand people use it every year for fishing, swimming and relaxing. If the river were to become polluted by the waste from a factory, what would be the consequence? Substitute swimming pools, fishing facilities and possibly a park would have to be provided. If these cost £25 million to construct, then the river's value for recreation would also amount to £25 million.

Naturally, these calculations have their snags but we shall come back to those when dealing with the functions of nature. However, even treating nature as a capital which yields interest, its value cannot always be expressed in monetary terms. In many cases it is impossible. We only make the comparison because this is the only way in which most people can get any idea of what nature is worth in economic terms.

Nevertheless, the principle is important. In current economic theory and practice, raw materials and energy are converted into products, and finally become waste matter. In this case a *supply* is only used once, although a significant part of it belongs to the natural capital. Most economists do not recognise this fact. They feel that the time when the supply will be exhausted lies so far ahead that we do not need to worry about it.

On the other hand, an economic system which takes the interests of nature into account works with a *flow* of materials, which is inexhaustible when the conditions for maintaining the natural capital are complied with. This flow is unfailing and delivers a constant but limited supply *as long as* nature is not encroached upon. A wood provides the same amount of timber every year, except when trees are felled at a higher rate than the annual growth of the wood. The sea supplies a constant supply of proteins in the form of fish, but this ceases when more fish are caught than the stocks can replenish.

This principle holds good for every part of nature. Sometimes such parts are called *functions*, that is they have many uses. But the usefulness for man is not always clear. It is not easy, for example, to see the value for man of a particular bird or a particular butterfly. But this does not mean that the creatures in question are useless. In itself, perhaps a butterfly seems to be only as insignificant as a little screw in the mechanism of an aeroplane, which does not have very much intrinsic value either. But the butterfly and the screw do have something in common: they are parts of a total system which would fall apart if those small components were not there. And so the small components of nature must not be ignored when we talk about the large ones.

above The estuary is a spawning ground for myriad life forms in the chain. But it needs to be unpolluted to keep its function

below A water-purification plant. Humankind has already had to revert to other means to maintain its clean water after degrading the environment

above A tree in the city, magnificent to see but not always appreciated for the way it keeps the air clean and for the oxygen it provides

left An air-purification filter in Paris. An ugly and expensive way to imitate the function of the tree–and far less efficient. The experiment failed.

Five. The Use and Misuse
of Nature

*'Human history more and more becomes a
race between education and catastrophe'.*
H. G. Wells

Nature is used in all kinds of ways. Sometimes consciously, sometimes unconsciously: often it is misused. Always it is used to further man's purposes. And because its *functions* are essential for the satisfaction of man's needs they are economically significant.

Nature's ruination is not always caused by such obvious operations as the direct destruction of woodlands or the extermination of animals. Human activities such as industry and use of transport and buildings also damage the earth and the atmosphere, disseminate poisons, make a noise and reduce the life-expectancies of plants, animals and people. Up to now economists have hardly ever taken these things into account when calculating the cost of an activity. It was not considered necessary. They are referred to as *external effects* (as if to remove responsibility for them) and then ignored when costs and revenues are calculated. External effects can be either negative or positive. A positive external effect for example, is the beauty of a tulip field in bloom, although the tulip field was not planned for this purpose. Negative external effects are those in which production has caused some kind of damage. The ease with which economists have dismissed the unpleasant side-effects of production in the past results from the commonly-held idea that natural resources are inexhaustible, and therefore may be used by everyone, and for nothing. Luckily, this is out-of-date. It is now a platitude that the world is limited in size and has a limited bearing-capacity.

Another problem is that the number of people is increasing so quickly that the area available per head is getting rapidly smaller. It is estimated that in 1600 there were 500 million people. By 1900 the population had grown to 1600 million, and now it has reached 4000 million. In the next thirty years the population will probably double for, in the interim, 120 people are born every minute. One difficulty is that those areas where people like to live are very often the same areas in which wild plants and animals find the most suitable conditions. That may be expected, for man too is a part of nature. But unfortunately, in global terms the regions where people are squeezing animals and plants out of existence are comparatively small. 'Unfortunately', because it means they compete for space. No less than 78% of the globe is covered by water or ice, 5% is, to us, uninhabitable desert, and what remains is often too cold, too hot, too steep, too high or too wet to be lived in. Nearly everywhere, it appears that the demand for more ground for housing, transport, industry or agriculture is at nature's expense.

When some activity or other makes a demand on nature's stores, the same stores cannot be used for other purposes. For example, a river may be used for the discharge of industrial waste water. Depending on the type of waste, micro-organisms in the river may break down the effluent, but they need time to work and so a stretch of the river becomes polluted. Nobody can swim there any more. The fact that nature has the task of treating waste here prevents it from fulfilling its recreation function. The river cannot exercise both functions simultaneously. Hueting speaks about 'competing functions' and this concept is useful because it helps make clear the fact that mother nature cannot go on taking care of us for ever.

With the exception of a number of chemical substances (such as DDT) a river can biologically break down a large part of the filth poured into it. However, a river's capacity for dealing with pollution is limited. If too much waste water is dischargd into it, putrefaction and stench result, because the purifying organisms in the water are unable to cope with the quantity. So there is a 'loss of function'. The same principle applies to nature's potential for purifying air or making recreation possible. How then, can such disturbing and expensive negative external effects be remedied? Some of them can be put right by the ones who caused them in the first place. Factories after all can purify their own waste water, smoke and so on. They can be forced to do so by legislation, and this has proved to be the best way of preventing negative external effects up to now. When a factory has to foot the bill for its own external effects it incurs expenses which send up the price of the finished product. The cost is passed on to the consumer and, if the price is too high, and the product not essential, the demand will drop and there will be less inclination to manufacture the product.

A second possibility is that someone other than the factory may counter the negative external effects, usually the government. In current methods of accounting, this has a strange influence on the way a factory's output is expressed in the national product. When a factory discharges its waste water into a river and the government builds a plant down-stream to purify the polluted water, then not only the output of the factory but also the building of the purification plant are added to the GNP. This is illogical. For the cost of repairs for damage inflicted – i.e. the cost of building and operating the purification plant – is obviously expenditure.

When a piece of ground is used for human structures, nature has been banished from it for the time being. Before making inroads into our remaining stocks of natural areas, we ought to be quite certain that the factory, road, airfield or whatever it may be really does have a lasting value. This is usually taken for granted. All that concrete and steel seems to have an eternal life! Limits to the useful life of a building development are often not considered in taking the decision to build. It is assumed that what is all right today will still be all right in twenty, forty or eighty years time.

With all production, no matter what product or what

undertaking may be concerned, the first economic problem is whether the capital invested can yield a certain margin of profit. If not, then the undertaking concerned cannot carry on. It does not matter whether that capital is provided by one person, a group of people (shareholders) or by the government; it always has to be kept intact, unless there are continuous attempts to make up the deficiencies by means of subsidies. The margin of profit on capital comes from what is left when the product is sold, and after all the costs have been deducted. These costs make up the greater part of the selling price. They are: the price of the raw materials, packaging, wages, salaries, energy, maintenance, depreciation on buildings and machinery, travelling expenses, transport and the profits for wholesaler and retailer. The profit on the capital represents only a small proportion, and so is vulnerable to fluctuations in the other costs. In order to ensure that money is available to pay the interest on the capital, the turnover and profit of the undertaking have to be estimated with accuracy. This is difficult, because there are many uncertain factors. It is clear that the entrepreneur has to look far ahead and estimate how much of his article is likely to be used and what share of the market it will be able to capture. He has to guess how producers, consumers and authorities at home and abroad will behave; and whether someone else may be able to hit on a cheaper production method. Or will something, yet to be invented, cause another product to become more attractive? Or will his product go out of fashion, perhaps? And will importing countries slap on an import duty?

In all production, the rule is that a proportionally small margin of profit is obtained against the total value of the end-product. This amount is decisive for the question of whether the business will pay its way. This minimal sum will be earned on the basis of expectations which are extremely difficult to forecast. It is not for nothing that an indemnification for risks run is included in the producers charges.

There are many signs that in the stagnating economic situation of around 1975, the expectations of entrepreneurs were based on patterns of thought and living which belonged to the years of economic triumph, rather than to those of a society which had, in the meantime, learned to live and think differently. Industrial developments and production operate more and more at the expense of a scanty supply of space and natural resources, and thus a scanty supply of economic goods. So a decision to establish an industry, without bearing in mind its consequences for nature and the locality, may be a decision to jeopardize the existence of nature there for the sake of goods that may be quite inessential.

The stagnating growth of production does indicate that there is little need for many of the articles manufactured. But because the need for nature can hardly be made visible on a market of supply and demand, another signal is required in order to perceive the need. Inquiries and opinion polls and, above all, the enormous increase in the members of environmental conservation organizations show us that the 'economic subjects' (people) have a growing awareness of their need for environmental products. An entrepreneur or government which denies this and sets up an industry in an area of exceptional natural value is aiding and abetting the decline of prosperity.

Flamingo Island

Recent developments on Bonaire show how narrow are the limits within which industrial prognoses often operate, and how dangerous this can be for nature. On this Caribbean island there is a great desire to build up a tourist industry, but it is difficult to get it under way. In common with 'our' island in the North Sea, the advantage which Bonaire has over many other tourist centres is its natural beauty; and it has one particular attraction – the world of flamingos. Aruba, Bonaire and Curaçao – the Leeward Islands – are situated about a hundred kilometres north of Venezuela. The tropical sun beats down on them and they are fanned by a refreshing trade wind from the Caribbean sea. The oil industry, which processes products from Venezuela, has brought a good deal of activity to Curaçao and Aruba, but only came to Bonaire recently. Many years ago, Bonaire had a considerable amount of vegetation. Amerigo Vespucci wrote about it as 'the island with the Brazilian wood'. In the days of the West Indies Company, the Dutch cut down this costly 'dye' wood and prisoners in the house of correction (the rasp house) in Amsterdam pulverized it into a red dye for the cloth industry. As in other parts of the world, the goats and hatchets soon got the upper hand. Bonaire is now an island with very little vegetation, where only experts can trace the remains of an interesting past. Wonderful coral reefs lie in the blue sea around the island, surrounded by throngs of fishes like something out of a fairy tale. Underwater hunting was popular here for a long time but, like everywhere else, it has decimated so many animal varieties that it has had to be stopped. And then, there are the flamingos.

The travel bureaux call Bonaire 'Flamingo Island'. Tourists can catch the plane to Flamingo airport and laze on Flamingo beach. In the little old streets they can buy ashtrays with flamingos on them, and flamingo spoons and whiskey glasses decorated with flamingos. The magnificent rose-coloured birds have a greater appeal to the imagination than most other creatures. This is not only because the birds succeed in living in such inhospitable conditions that it has required biologists to explain how they manage it. The main reason is their remarkable pink colour and their stately form, about which Anthony Donker wrote:

'Flamingos, little flares, in the kingdom
of the dead, unquenchable bonfires.
But when they rise up a flame swirls up
out of the grey salt marsh on high
as if the flock flew towards a new life.'

Donker's last sentence may be more significant than he ever imagined. It is possible that the last flock will leave Bonaire one day for good to look for a new place to live.

South Bonaire is flat and low. It used to be a beautiful landscape, with curiously-shaped low-lying areas around the

Pekelmeer (Brine Lake), into which sea water crept through all kinds of tortuous channels. This evaporated so quickly in the sun and wind that sea salt was deposited, and people collected it in primitive salt pans. One of the few animals which can tolerate a high concentration of salt is the brine shrimp, whose larvae and pupae attach themselves to the lower surfaces of stones. The flamingos can sift out the larvae and pupae with manoeuvres of their down-curved beaks. Jan Rooth, a research worker, has estimated that the 1500 flamingos he counted in the Pekelmeer consumed 48 million pupae every day.

When the flamingos are breeding they build a nest of mud. This is no more than a bare mound with a dip on the top in which a single egg is laid. The solitary chick has to be fed large quantities until it is about four months old. It seems remarkable that so many young birds survive the very hot and salty conditions in which they live.

Only six varieties of flamingos are known in the world. The Caribbean flamingo, which lives on Bonaire and along the north coast of South America, is only found in one or two other places. A hundred years ago, there were 100,000 of them, scattered over dozens of nesting places. There are about 60,000 flamingos alive now, which means that there are about 15,000 breeding pairs. About 10,000 of these live on the Bahamas and Cuba, 3,000 pairs in Mexico, 100 pairs in the Galapagos archipelago and 2,500 pairs on Bonaire.

There was a serious disturbance of the latter in 1943 when aircraft flew too low over the colony, after which the birds failed to breed for six years. From this time on, the colony remained fairly stable.

Until comparatively recently salt extraction was carried out in a primitive fashion and never did much harm to the birds. But things have changed. In 1962, at the request of the Board of Government of Bonaire, the Central Institute for Industrial Development in The Hague made an investigation into the possibility of making salt-extraction more profitable. According to their report, salt-extraction on a fairly small scale would show a profit. But their recommendations were not followed. New proposals were made; this time with a report from the International Salt Company, which asked the Board of Government for permission to exploit all the southern part of Bonaire, including the Pekelmeer. This new study showed that a good profit would be made on a much larger scale development with an investment of about £3.6 million (about $6.5 million). The Pekelmer would be connected to the sea by an open channel. Water from the channel would increase the concentration of salt, as it passed through a series of modern salt pans. In the final stage much greater quantities of salt would be extracted. The industry itself would provide jobs for between eighty and a hundred and fifty workers. The Netherlands would build a landing-stage for the transport of the salt at a cost of about £312,000.

Members of Parliament and the Natural Sciences Study Club for Surinam and the Netherlands Antilles, pleaded the cause of the flamingos. But the new plans were pushed through. The agreement was signed in 1966. The newly-formed Antilles International Salt Company pledged itself to consider the interests of the flamingos 'as far as possible' and even set aside the sum of £50,000 to provide for this objective. A group of nature conservationists was to have a say in the framing of the plans. It was estimated that there would be an annual output of 400,000 tons of raw industrial salt after four years. Two hundred people would be given jobs during the construction period and after that there would be a permanent staff of sixty local workmen, with another sixty temporary helpers when the salt was being scooped up and shipped. It all looked very promising.

What became of it all? Over ten years later, the annual salt production is between 150000 and 200000 tons, and fifty-one people are employed. The salt-extracting industry is not doing so well as was predicted. Too little salt is being produced, for the newly-built salt-pans are leaking because of underground connections with the sea: and there are fresh plans once more to change the course of the water completely. Marketing possibilities and freight prices have been disappointing too. The fact is, that none of the expectations have been realised, nor has a reasonable profit been made on the capital invested.

With the flamingos, too, things have not worked out according to plan. They did, indeed, take over the area set aside for them as a breeding ground. But the amount of food available for them has not been sufficient. A thick layer of gypsum crystals has formed here and there on the bottom of the new salt pans, which were to have been a flamingos' paradise. This layer of gypsum hinders the development of the larvae and pupae of the brine shrimp. So the birds are forced to look around for other food, such as small crustaceans, and it remains to be seen whether these will be abundant enough.

Flamingos are flaunted as the visiting card of Bonaire. They are the trade-mark under which the island is sold on the travel market. And the tourist industry is one of the few sources of income on the island. However, statistics for 1975 show that the five hotels on Bonaire only had 146 rooms between them, while there were eight to ten times as many on Aruba and Curaçao. There is plenty of room for more on Bonaire. The point at which the number of tourists would become a threat to nature conservation has – if their activities are kept within reasonable bounds – not yet been reached. Every hotel room occupied means one and a third jobs for the hotel business, and that doesn't include the restaurants, shops and casino. The fifty-one jobs provided by the salt-extracting industry are of minor importance in comparison. If the stream of tourists subsides because there are fewer flamingos, then any advantage that the salt-extraction industry gave to the island will soon turn into a disadvantage.

Perhaps the lag-effect of the wave of visitors will temporarily sustain the belief that some hotels, beaches, night clubs and swimming pools are all that Bonaire needs for its tourist industry. But one can find these anywhere. When 'Flamingo Island' no longer has any flamingos the attraction will not be so strong.

This is not an isolated incident; parallels can be found in most industrial countries. It merely serves to demonstrate that the road to prosperity is not always reached via increased production. This route may even lead away from prosperity.

Heron's nesting ground before the destruction of the habitat

Six. The Functions of Nature

'Man and nature are one and the same. The sooner we conservationists accept this fact, the sooner our concerns and aspirations will become part of the mainstream of human affairs'.

Russell Train. 1967

Nature's existence ensures in all kinds of ways that the needs of economy, health, agriculture and recreation are all catered for. Without nature there would be no production, no art, no science and, in fact, no civilization. All this has been said so often and with so much verbosity, and so little attention paid to it, that one begins to suspect most people have no idea of the functions of nature. That is why we list here the most important of them:

1 *Nature regulates the stability of the environment and the climate*

This is one of the main functions on which so many others depend. Healthy soil, clean water and a stable climate are among man's primary requisites for living conditions. Plant diseases and plagues should not occur too often, neither should floods, nor erosion. If nature is in a state of balance, a rare occurrence these days, then it controls these things. It produces clean water, purifies the air and 'disposes' of waste; it keeps the soil healthy and in place and, in some places, fertile; and it keeps bacteria and harmful organisms in a web of biological filaments called the 'natural balance'. All this is done freely, until something in the system is broken down. When this happens there is usually an attempt made to imitate the function by using our modern technology which costs a great deal of money. Often it cannot be imitated at all, and a function is lost.

2 *Nature supplies resources and raw materials*
Modern communities need a supply of many raw materials: protein and starch, drinking water, minerals, fuel, wood, medicaments and new agricultural strains. Nature can provide a constant flow of these products as long as its productive capacities are not encroached on. Responsible hunting and fishing can be conducive to a constant flow of animal protein, and responsible forestry to a constant flow of timber products and cellulose. With the help of the pool of genetic material provided by nature, it is possible to change the cultivated strains of plants or domestic animals to suit our agricultural requirements and micro-organisms can prove (and have proved in the past) to be unsuspected aids to medicine. Nature also provides us with the means to obtain hydro-electricity.

3 *Nature is a source of scientific data*
Without nature it is almost impossible to practise or apply science. Biology, geology, architecture, chemistry, physics and even literature, economics and psychology depend, either partly or completely, on the possibilities afforded by nature. Knowledge of nature leads to familiarity with stabilizing and disturbing factors in both natural and social systems.

4 *Nature is essential for mental and bodily health*
People pursue leisure activities: they go cycling, walking, camping, hiking, fishing, swimming, sailing, diving; they go off on day trips and relax in a hundred other ways. The advantages of this recreation in nature's surroundings are not only that many people (and countries) derive an income from it but also that those who recreate benefit directly, e.g. through improved health and a relief of tension.

5 *Nature is a source of inspiration for culture*
Without nature, life would be very dull indeed. Nature is a source of inspiration for painting, films, television programmes, architecture, advertising, fashion, industrial de-

sign, dancing, folklore, costumes, popular art, education, sport and games. There is hardly any province of culture to which nature does not give shape or inspiration. Economically then, it is invaluable, for nature is involved either directly or indirectly with almost the whole of our social system.

Seven. Natural Balance

'The wind grew stronger. The rain crust broke and the dust lifted up out of the fields and drove grey plumes into the air like sluggish smoke.'
John Steinbeck in *The Grapes of Wrath*

Ecological concepts

As capital, nature can only yield interest when it is in a state of balance. But most people have no idea of what is meant by this, and there are some odd conceptions of what nature is. Planners designate narrow strips of vegetation between roads or oil tanks as 'nature areas', even though only nettles, elders, willows and couch grass may be growing there. Is this nature? Certainly it may be a collection of natural plants and animals but this does not mean that there is any natural diversity or balance.

Like any other capital, nature has to be maintained in good condition. Otherwise in the long term it is of no use to humankind. An ordinary capital good, such as a building or a ship, is maintained by human labour, by repairing it or painting it. This does not apply to nature, for which the ideal state of affairs is to be left completely undisturbed, so that it maintains its own balance. But this is impossible because very little unspoilt nature remains, so that the best course is, through wise management, to give the self-regulating processes in nature as much opportunity as possible to operate.

The science which studies these processes is called ecology. Ecologists investigate the relations between living creatures and their animate and inanimate environment.

This book deals with the relationship between economics

and ecology. Therefore, to understand the subject, one needs to know some of the terms used in ecology and its more elementary rules, besides those of economics. Communities of plants and animals (including human beings) in a certain area are called *ecosystems*. An ecosystem can be small in size, such as a willow on which all kinds of small plants and animals live; large, such as the Wadden Sea; or very large, such as the entire biosphere – the area inhabited by living things on earth and in the atmosphere. So nature consists of millions of small ecosystems which, together, make up one large ecosystem. The inaminate part of an ecosystem consists of the water, earth and air and is called the *abiotic milieu*. But even under natural conditions ecosystems are not static arrangements of plants, animals and inaminate material. They develop from primitive stages to mature systems in a process called *succession*. Here the self-regulating capacity of a system increases as that system becomes fully developed. The first stage is simple, relatively unstable and is called the *pioneer stage*. The final stage in a succession is complex, more or less stable and is called the *climax community*. However, an environmental change, whether caused by humans (e.g. a fire) or by nature (e.g. a drought) can soon bring the development back to a simple system.

A major difference between the two extremes is that, in the early stages, the production of *biomass* (the total mass of all the plants and animals) is used for the development of the system, while in the late stage it is used for its maintenance.

The *diversity* of a system, that is the number of different species in it, is generally low early on in a succession and is large in the late stages.

The *biological level of organisation* is indicated by the size of the organisms present, and the demands which they make on their environment. For the pioneers in a system are generally small plants such as lichens and micro-organisms. The deciduous trees of the climax community are obviously more demanding of nutrients. The *food chain*, that is, the route by which nutrients circulate through the system, is fairly short and simple in the early stages, and becomes both longer and more complex. In every biological system plants and animals compete with one another for a place, for space, for nutrition, light, air and all the things they need to survive, so that early in the development of a system there is a rapid growth in the number of individuals of species present. But in the late stages of a succession this constant selection pressure will maintain a constant level of the species present of the most suitable quality only. There will be more species and fewer individuals of each. The most important thing is that the development of a natural succession from start to climax takes a long *time*.

The time needed to develop fully varies with the situation and the physical environment (water, mountains, marsh, steppe). A swiftly-flowing stream may perhaps require only a few years, a tidal area such as the Wadden Sea in Holland, some decades, but a tropical forest would certainly take several centuries. It is inevitably a lengthy process, and this fact is of the greatest importance in resisting the idea that there could be no objection to using that odd patch of heath, this wood or that stretch of mudflats for industrial purposes. 'We can always create another area like this somewhere else, can't we?'

No, we can't: natural successions cannot be speeded up; neither by technology nor even by the minister with an item for 'replacing nature' in his budget. Political pronouncements on these lines are meaningless. They have as much value as the proposal to suspend the law of gravity for a while.

What, then, is the nature of succession? In the pioneer stage nature is still unbalanced. An example of such an area (common in the Netherlands), is where sand has been dumped on the ground on a new building site. If some time elapses before building is started, all kinds of plants establish themselves on the sand. These are always the same ones – fleabane, milkwort, silverweed, St. John's wort, plantain, sorrel, various species of grasses and other 'weeds'. The soil (sand in this case) is poor in nutrients to begin with, few species of plants are present, and not many species of animals find it attractive. Few birds live there and only a small number of insect species. So both the flora and fauna of a pioneer area like this are poor.

However few species there are living in a pioneer area, they are present in large numbers, which makes their community vulnerable. When there is a sudden disturbance, for example a great change of temperature, or the sudden onset of a disease, all of the individuals of a species may be affected and thus the species which depend on them – e.g. for food. And there are *fluctuations in the populations* of flora and fauna. This can be shown with a line (figure 2) which represents the succession, or series, with the course of time.

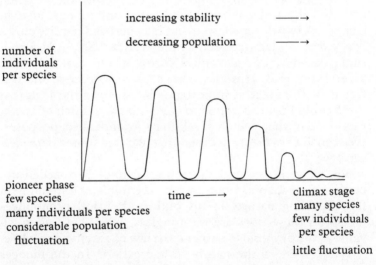

figure 2 Succession scale

With the passing of time the richness of species diversity increases, while the fluctuations in population decrease. In the climax system they are minimal, with a maximum stability. Of course, this does not mean that suddenly things are at a standstill. Equilibrium is not a state of rest but a dynamic condition in which the multiplicity of processes, all interlinking with each other, means that the state of the system as a whole remains more or less constant. Figures 3 and 4 illustrate the development. The perimeter square in figure 3 represents an area in which the natural succession has just begun. Only four species of plants are found in this example, A, B, C and D. If the system is now affected by a disease in species B, for example, then a large part of the area, a quarter in this example, will be altered very rapidly.

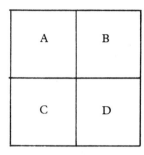

figure 3 Pioneer system

In the course of time the ground becomes covered with plant remains. Humus is formed in which all kinds of minute organisms can live, and the poor soil gradually becomes more fertile. Other plants are then able to grow. And this process continues with more plants coming in, growing and dying and the ground becoming more fertile until eventually there is a large number of species, each of which is represented by comparatively few specimens. A climax system has come into being, and A, B, C and D are now accompanied by E to Y (figure 4). If the same disease now affects plant B only 1/25th of the whole system is disturbed, and it does not become unbalanced. One can compare this to a ship with many watertight bulk-heads. One leak does not make the ship sink. A pioneer system is a ship without similar provision.

Because of this great variety of plant species and of the wealth of soil life (micro-organisms), many insects, birds and other species of animals can also thrive there. Here, too, the general rule is that a disturbance to one particular species of animal is unlikely to affect the system as a whole in a climax community.

A	B	C	D	E
F	G	H	I	J
K	L	M	N	O
P	Q	R	S	T
U	V	W	X	Y

figure 4 Climax system

But that is not an excuse for exterminating a species of animal. On the contrary, although such a simple conclusion is very apt to be drawn by people who seize on a single detail which is to their own advantage out of a complicated account, and then forget the rest. The result of the disappearance of that single species of animal is that the climax system loses a small part of its diversity. The species does not stand alone but is linked up with the rest of the system. With every species that is eliminated, the system shifts back along the succession line in the direction of the pioneer stage. A 'component' is lost. The fewer components, the more unstable the system becomes and the more *fluctuations* there will be. If one or two species of birds disappear today, a few plants tomorrow, a mammal next week and a bird of prey the week after that, then the climax community will be slightly affected over and over again by all these occurrences. But some species are so important that the result of their disappearance is a sudden jerk from climax to pioneer stage, while others cause this to a lesser degree. One can rarely, if ever, say with precision which those are. A good yard-stick for the stability, and thus for the constancy of the climax system, is usually the presence of the higher plant and animal species. As a rule, higher species of animals are situated at the end of a long food chain, and their presence tallies with the large number of varieties character-istic of such a long food chain. Higher species of plants only appear after development has progressed a long way and the lower species are established. These, the strong pioneer plants, fight a vanguard action, so to speak, to make the soil suitable for the higher species to grow. It is easy to keep this as a maxim, the more so because it is generally these higher species which have most to fear from man. Impoverishment of nature is nearly always the result of human interference. In an environment crowded with sparrows, starlings, pigeons, crows, sea-gulls, rats, mice, mosquitoes and flies, this process has already taken place. There is no question of a natural balance. Taking the short-term view, one can still cherish the illusion that when nature has been ousted or impoverished, progress has been made. Economists simply add up the sale of the capital with the income and cry out triumphantly that prosperity has increased and progress is made, because the National Income has grown. But poverty is sure to follow when a succeeding generation has to foot the bill for our present plenty.

We can illustrate this best with reference to agriculture. Is this in accord with nature or not? What factors ought agriculture to take into account if it is to obtain the largest possible yields and at the same time be ecologically re-sponsible? The line of reasoning followed above is the same. Metaphorically speaking, agriculture is little more than a piece of nature which has been tied up in a kind of strait-jacket for human advantage. Then how can we still profit from the advantages of the climax or 'stable' stage? And in regions where agriculture is carried on intensively what are the factors that will help the movement, as far as possible, towards the climax community, so as to make use of the power of resistance to disturbances characterizing such a system?

'These factors are mostly found in the environment surrounding the agricultural areas, provided that this still
possesses the characteristics of a climax system.

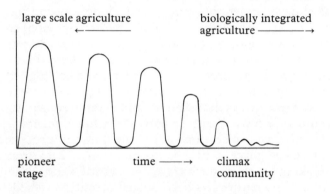

figure 5 Agriculture on the succession scale

Stretches of woodland can be such factors, and hedges and
banks of earth topped by bushes can also contribute.
Countless organisms, plants, trees, mammals and insects live
in these areas. They have a finely-meshed web of relationships with one another and with the non-living environment. This system can contribute towards a stable micro-
climate, a natural water supply, the limitation of pests and
diseases and so towards a type of agriculture which, if well-
planned, does not exhaust the soil, poison it or abandon it to
erosion. Hypermodern, large-scale, mechanized agriculture
pays very little heed to these naturally stabilizing resources.
Agriculture of this kind tends to shift towards the pioneer
stage on the succession scale, whereas a biologically-
integrated agriculture shifts the other way. This has varying
results (see figure 5). The fluctuations in 'safety' become

greater and greater when 'shifting to the left' on the scale. More monoculture, thus many individuals belonging to one species, is accompanied by the characteristics of the pioneer stage. While this can be favourable for production, it is naturally unfavourable for natural stability. So while there is the desired increase in agricultural yields, one also finds a greater susceptibility to disease and pests, because self-regulating functions disappear in proportion as agriculture is carried out further to the left on the scale.

The significance of natural balance is very obvious here. Because it is risky to carry out agriculture in the extreme pioneer stage, with the increased risk of diseases and pests becoming a problem, agriculture has to make concessions to the maximum possible amount of production which can be obtained there. It is true that farmers do try to shift as far as possible to the left on the scale, but then a point is reached at which they can go no further. Biologically-integrated agriculture opts for a smaller chance of diseases and pests becoming a problem, but a somewhat lower yield. Intensive agriculture, on the other hand, opts for large harvests and tries to hold diseases in check by chemical and other artificial means. With all this, it is almost impossible to estimate the economic value of a natural balance. The world's costs of pest control in agriculture run into tens of millions of dollars annually. Depending on time and place, it is possible to make agriculture 'less pioneer and more climax', and therefore less vulnerable to pests, without the yield suffering. *If it were possible* to do this optimally throughout the world, so that the need for artificial pest controls decreased and disappeared, then, as far as this function is concerned, the economic value of the natural climax system (i.e. the famous 'balance') would be equal to the capitalized value of the techno-chemical pest control, which would no longer be needed.

It is not so strange that a reasoning along these lines seems rather incredible at first sight. Large-scale, mechanized agriculture has grown at such a rapid rate that people are inclined to look on suggestions for other systems as romantic, exaggerated or useless. But this goes for *every* argument which casts doubt on the durability of the advantages which some technical innovation or other must produce. There is nothing romantic about the discovery of the properties of nature, and recording that certain technical inventions and applications are incompatible with those properties. Indeed, no matter how large the scale of modern agrarian technique may be and how unchangeable it may seem, these new ecological views may have to be adopted eventually. Accordingly, we now need to look for methods of practising agriculture in the framework of a more stable natural system, because the lack of them can lead to irremediable disaster.

Natural balance is a very complex affair, whose subtlety may never be quite understood. Even the global rules that we know vary from area to area, so that one can never talk of 'the' biological balance as if there were only one. It may be suggested that generally speaking, the vulnerability of the balance becomes greater as the climate becomes cooler and as the number of species per unit area decreases. It may also be suggested that a disturbance in the warmer climates is usually more dramatic, because the potential danger, in the form of harmful insects, viruses, and the like is greater there.

Rice cultivation past and present

That a natural balance can also be aided, to a certain extent, through the teamwork of agriculture with surrounding nature is shown by the example of rice cultivation. The wet paddy fields of such countries as Indonesia, the Philippines, Vietnam, Cambodia and Thailand represent one of the oldest agricultural methods in the world. The paddy fields of the island of Java are between a thousand and two thousand years old and are regarded as a fine example of naturally integrated agriculture. They are exceptional for, in spite of the high yields of rice, on the succession scale this cultivation is well on the way to being a climax system.

The climate is hot and humid and the soil is rich in minerals and nutrients. The water is abundant, and secured by the rich root system of the forests on the mountain slopes. The paddy fields are irrigated with this water, which brings some nutrients out of the forests. An ingenious, centuries-old system of dykes keeps the water and soil in place. And so swift and violent torrents of water (bandjirs), which wash away the precious humus, are not a risk.

The number of varieties of rice that are cultivated runs into hundreds. Every district has its own type. As a rule mildew and virus diseases only prey on one particular species, so that an infestation only affects one area, and there is never a wholesale shortage of food. These old species of rice have long, supple stalks and small ears. There are two harvests a year when the ears are cut off with a small knife and the stalks burnt. The ash returns to the soil to remain a part of the cycle. Larvae of the malaria mosquito are found in the water, and are eaten by little paddy fishes whose faeces contribute to the fertility of the soil. The little fishes are an essential protein supplement to the rice diet of the people, but are also eaten by small white egrets, found in every single paddy field. The egrets, in turn, provide additional nitrogen fertilization. Competition for the crop exists in the form of the rice-birds or Java sparrows, which peck at the grains of rice and are driven away with the help of strings of rattling and clapping contraptions, worked from small huts. All around and within the paddy fields, the black snake lives. He is the master ratcatcher, who has his own way of controlling the number of small rodents.

At least this is how it was for centuries that is until the Green Revolution came, bringing its dubious blessings. Rice cultivation changed and is threatened now.

The numerous old species of rice have been replaced by just a few new hybrids, called HYVs (High Yielding Varieties). This is so close to being a monoculture that a biological disturbance means that the whole system is out of balance. If a virus infestation of the rice occurs, enormous areas can be affected. Such infestations are controlled with toxic chemicals, the pesticides. These halt the spread temporarily, but the poison accumulates in the food chain, via the mosquito larvae, in insects and fishes. As a result the little egrets become poisoned by eating the fish and die or fail to breed. The rice-birds cannot tolerate the poison in the rice either, and are decimated. Rats, which eat the dead birds and the poisoned fish, are resistant to high concentrations of poison. However, the black snake which eats the rat is not and accumulates the poison. And as the black snake disappears, so the rats multiply explosively. But there are other problems. The HYVs have short, hard stalks, so that as much as possible of the energy taken in is converted into grains of rice and the stalks are reaped mechanically and taken away from the paddy fields. Rats could not climb up the old, long, weak stalks, but they can climb up the new short and strong ones and, in ever-increasing numbers, they devour the harvest. In addition there are now three harvests a year, which means that a heavier burden is put on the soil. To make matters worse, the forests in the surrounding hills are being felled and the rainwater pours down from the mountainsides onto the paddy fields. So the water is much poorer in nutrients than when it was taken up by the forest soil first. The resulting deficiency of nutrients in the water is compensated for by artificial fertilizer. Artificial fertilizer causes the remaining fish to disappear, because the paddy field is too rich in nutrients, which stimulate the growth of algae, and when these algae die they deprive the water of all its oxygen. Fish die in oxygen-free water, but not the malaria larva. Consequently the malaria mosquito can breed uncontrolled.

After many centuries of stable agriculture, through a unique system of co-operation with nature, the result of the change is leached-out soil, an increase of rats, malaria and hunger, Java now has 80 million inhabitants. In order to be able to feed the population, which is increasing by 2.5 million people annually, rice cultivation is being extended and modernized. Ostensibly, this has been successful so far, because rice production has increased. But the drawbacks are already becoming obvious. Yet people persist in travelling this road, which will lead to Java's becoming a desolate island before the end of this century. A waste land.

But what is the economic value of the natural balance on Java? Clearly, forests, black snakes and fishes all contributed in an important way to rice cultivation, and therefore to the economy of the population. However, it is impossible to assess their 'economic value' in money terms. The comparison we have made just gives an *indication*: the costs incurred for chemical pest control, compared with the lack of costs in the period of ecologically-integrated agriculture, taking the lower yields of that period into account, of course.

A similar indication can be given of the value of one important link in the balance of nature, a common songbird. A little creature weighing between fifteen and twenty grammes, and of which some thousands of species exist. All but a few of them are insect-eaters. One such songbird catches approximately 675 insects every day. And the daily energy consumption of an insect-eater weighing eighteen grammes is thirteen kilocalories (54340 joules), which is provided by thirteen grammes of insects. Thus the small bird eats more than four and a half kilos of insects every year. So one ordinary songbird gets rid of about 100,000 insects annually each weighing about one twentieth of a gramme. If one assumes that this is useful work, then the bird has some economic importance. No economist could deny this. What is the value of this work? We asked some experts in the field of pest control what it would cost to get rid of 100,000 insects a year, without using insecticides. Apparently the question was confusing, for it was impossible to obtain a straight-forward answer. And so we asked a nature conservationist to try to make the estimate for us.

We readily admit that this estimate is absurd, because the efficiency of the bird cannot be imitated by anything or anyone. But let us just imagine, for the sake of estimation, that one person is able to deputize for the bird. Assuming that this fly and mosquito-catcher travels around by bicycle, the cost of this will amount to about about £7,500 a year. If this method does not work (and it does not), then, perhaps groups of people would have to work to comb the catchment area with butterfly nets in search of insects – incidentally trampling that area flat in the process. If the vegetation were ruined, during the extermination of the insects, the calculation of costs would have to include this damage. And so on.

In fact the postulation of the international ornithologist Peter Conder, that the small bird has no economic value, is just as foolish as our calculation, which would have to stipulate the exact sum of money involved. This is not so important, because the only controversial question would be, to what extent is the elimination of insect pests a useful, and therefore economically valuable task. Considering that the world spent over £16,000 million (30,000 million dollars) on chemical pesticides and other controls in 1973, it appears to be a task of considerable priority.

Nature and agriculture must co-exist

We do not mean to say that the short-term advantage of chemical technology and modern intensive methods of agriculture is always wrong. The character of a community can be such that, for reasons of ethics and politics, or just plain survival, it is vital to produce much food very quickly. The move towards an ecological balance between agriculture and nature can be sought in later years.

In a country such as Israel, for example, any other sequence would have been impossible, because the course of a natural succession there would have taken too long – perhaps centuries. With the help of chemical and mechanical methods, agriculture has almost literally been started from the grass-roots. Now that there is some vegetation including trees and there are better water cycles, the basis has been laid for development towards more biologically-integrated methods. If this fact is neglected then, in the long run, things will go wrong. For the attunement of agriculture with nature is one of the primary conditions necessary for a lasting stability of agriculture and food production. Certainly modern, large-scale agriculture pays little attention to these vital principles. But this is no wonder, for it is all too tempting to believe that techno-chemical aids can achieve absolute victory over pests, diseases and, thus, over hunger. Overcropping in the modern sense replaces the ignorant overcropping of years gone by almost unnoticeably. In those days, biological and agricultural principles were poorly understood. Knowledge of soil structure or of the interdependence of living organisms was either totally lacking or insufficiently widespread. It is true that, in some places, agricultural systems based on experience and tradition have evolved, without harming the balance of nature or even in harmony with it. But these are still too limited in area to be significant, when compared with the wholesale denudation and burning which has been going on for centuries. Because agriculture is usually carried out on land which – it has been beautifully expressed – 'has been wrested from nature', it is often thought that nature and agriculture are each other's enemies. But this need not be the case, for they cannot do without one another. It is not necessary to make a choice between the existence only of woods and natural areas without agriculture or only of endless fields without woodlands. The issue is one of maintaining an interplay of factors to ensure that agriculture can be continued without showing unpleasant side-effects or losing productivity; as demonstrated by the centuries-old cultivation of rice.

Plainly a great deal of food has to be produced for a rapidly growing world population. Agriculture requires an adequate layer of good topsoil, sufficient pure water, and healthy crops that will yield enough. Nature is indispensable for all these things but whether wild areas should be situated close to or far from the fields depends on all kinds of factors; it depends on the climate for example, on the quality of the humus already present and on whether the land is mountainous. In the Netherlands, with its mild maritime climate, where the sun never burns down for long and the rain usually falls softly on flat polders with fertile clay or peat soil, rich in humus, where there is an adjustable water table, the inhabitants will be inclined to think that they can do quite well without nature. That this is a mistake is only clear in the long run, in

contradistinction to tropical countries, where a mistake of
this kind is very swiftly punished.

One cannot do without forests in mountainous areas
because any humus present there would otherwise be leached
out. In regions where drought and torrential rains alternate, it
is always dangerous to leave too much of the ground exposed,
for then the topsoil disappears quickly. Then there is the fact
that healthy crop strains are essential. And the health of the
plants is closely related to their closeness to nature in the
vicinity.

The dynamic relationships, the complicated, interdependent processes in which both wild and cultivated plants have
to live, are steadily becoming clearer; but, strangely, nothing
whatever is being done to apply this knowledge. Most of
those countries which still possess vast areas of forests are not
attempting to manage them sensibly by leaving parts untouched, but exploiting them right down to the last tree.
Apparently, keeping the soil in place and the prevention of
erosion are not thought to be important. The long-term
interests stand in the way of the short-term interest of
commerce so far as governments and industrial enterprises
are concerned.

Woodlands around the Mediterranean have already disappeared. Today, the rain forests of South America, Africa and
South-east Asia are disappearing. These forests used to be
chopped down with hatchets and set on fire. Any remaining
vegetation was cropped short by goats. But, these days, the
forests are disappearing by means of mechanical felling and
with the help of particularly potent chemical pesticides. And
once the trees have gone, the rest follows automatically as we
explained in the section on *Vanishing Habitats*. If you are
lucky, a scanty grass vegetation takes possession of what was
once a jungle. Often you are not lucky and there is not even
that. Only the deserts of sand and stone remain; they have
been hidden for thousands of years, waiting for the inspection
of those who refuse to believe what short-sighted actions can
lead to.

In the nineteen thirties large areas of America were swept

by dust storms. In John Steinbeck's *The Grapes of Wrath* there is a breathtaking account of the dreadful conditions in the 'Dustbowl'. The over-harvesting of the vast prairies of the Middle West led to millions of tons of topsoil being, literally, blown away, in the years between 1933 and 1937. For days, sometimes for weeks, the day became as dark as night because of this. The dreams of thousands of free farmers were blown away in clouds of dust that were kilometres long and hundreds of metres high. The exhausted soil, badly harvested and badly cultivated, disappeared. It was a nightmare, beginning with mismanagement of the soil and ending with the exploitation of the farmers, who were forced to keep on negotiating fresh mortgages. Finally, only dilapidated farms were left in a desert of sand. A cynical anecdote tells how a despairing farmer went to a bank in a neighbouring town to plead for an umpteenth mortgage on his land. Just then another cloud of dust went flying through the streets, and the bank manager said, 'No sir, I can't give you another mortgage on your property. Just take a look through the window; it's blowing past right now'.

A similar fate befell the plains of Kazakstan in the 'fifties. According to the five-year plan then in force, the grassy steppes of this vast Russian land would become transformed into fields of waving grain. The land was brought under cultivation, but nature had not been taken into account and the soil was leached away by the rain and disappeared via the rivers towards the sea. In the dry summers the wind carried the rest away in great clouds of dust.

Formerly, something similar had happened in the countries around the Mediterranean. The most important cause of the deforestation here was the demand for wood. At one time, luxuriant forests grew on the now dessicated plateaux and mountainsides of Spain, Greece, Lebanon, Sicily and North Africa. The timber was used for building cities and temples and, later, especially for shipbuilding. The most ancient temples of the Carthaginians and Phoenicians and also of the Greeks and Romans were made of wood. And only when the wood was exhausted were stone temples built. From the form

of the stone pillars with their grooves, one can still see that
tree trunks were first to serve as supporting pillars. The long,
vertical grooves were borrowed from the bark of trees. King
Solomon had an army of a hundred thousand slaves con-
tinuously at work cutting down the cedar forests on the slopes
of the Lebanon. Generations of rulers came along after him to
complete this felling. So now only a pitiful remnant still
stands in a closely guarded reserve. Most of the regions round
the Mediterranean are bare and infertile now. Fertile soil
changed into desert. But the reverse is taking place in Israel;
there the desert is being driven back and changed into fertile
soil. This is happening with the help of labour forces,
machinery, irrigation projects and such aids as artificial
fertilizer, pesticides and fibrous materials to hold the soil in
place.

It costs money to conquer the desert. When the first harvest
festival is being celebrated on the new land, one can add up
the costs per hectare of making the desert blossom again. The
following can be gleaned from publications of the Israeli
forestry commission: the planting of trees can be looked on as
a first step in reclamation. Only when a forest has been
standing for a long time does the prospect of using parts of it
for agriculture look favourable. Cultivating the soil, planting
and taking care of young saplings during the first year of
growth, requires between 150 and 200 working days per
person per hectare. For example, if ten men are at work, it will
take them twenty days. If the terrain is suitable for working
with mechanical tools, the number of working days per
person is reduced to between thirty and thirty-five but
tractors have to be used then for fifteen days. However, these
are only the planting costs. In addition there is the construction of roads and fences to be accounted for, with all the
other provisions. Even then, these are only the direct costs.
Other large outlays are needed to prepare and supervise all
these activities.

These expenses give some idea of the value which nature
has as a protector against erosion. Without the erosion-
promoting activities of humans in bygone years, these outlays

would not have been necessary.

So here is another example of the human destruction of natural, environmental capital. If the annual yield per hectare of the ground is the interest, the capital can be estimated from this. With a 5% interest rate, the capital is twenty times as much. Here it is a question of thousands of millions of dollars vanishing into thin air all over the world. The leaders of a country would not readily tolerate this sort of destruction of capital in the form of buildings and man-made goods. Why then is it allowed to happen to nature?

Eight. Wonders Do Cease

'The first rule of intelligent tampering is to preserve all the pieces'.

Aldo Leopold

Tropical Forests: a secret world

Of all natural areas surely the forest is the most beautiful. There is nothing on earth that can compare with the green loveliness, the suspense, the mystery and the inscrutable character of the forest. Not one tree or plant, not a branch, not even a leaf is exactly like another. No sound resembles the one before, no gradation of colour is so surprising as in the forest or, more particularly, in the primeval forest.

Anyone who has set foot in the primeval forest will never forget this green hell or this green paradise. In literature, the primeval forest is exulted in, feared, defied and desecrated. Somerset Maugham describes the glory and the downfall of the temporary, strange white inhabitants of the hot equatorial forests, who become deranged there or enslaved to the forest and do not want to return to civilization. In Burrough's books, Tarzan the ape-man swings from tree to tree as 'the return to nature' personified. In the eighteenth century, 'le bon sauvage' (the 'noble savage') makes his appearance in literature; he is the romanticised ideal man, who dwells in the green paradises around the equator, and who was a fixed feature of the western dream about nature for two hundred years.

An end has now come to this flight of romanticism. The colonial era, and with it the yearning for the hot tropics, is now over. But what remains is the misunderstanding – the nonsense which is continually being written about the tropical forest. Many of the writers have only seen the edge of the jungle, which has already been possessed by bamboo and other such plants which would have no chance in the primeval forests. They do not know what it looks like from the inside and the virgin forest is always different from what one thinks. It is not all so impenetrable as it is often depicted. Only about one per cent of the sunlight reaches the ground, and there are very few plants which can grow in that semi-darkness. On the ground it is always damp and there is no wind. The torrential rains cannot reach the soil and the water drips from leaf to leaf.

Because of the upright stems we are inclined to see a forest as being composed of vertical elements. The forest is often compared with gothic cathedrals. But in a tropical forest, where the forms of life are determined by light intensity and humidity, the community consists of a number of horizontal layers. The highest level is taken up by the dominant forest giants which are characteristic of a primeval forest. These trees are between thirty-five and seventy metres high. The next storey down is made up of the crowns of other species of trees and the canopy of palms and lianas.

Lower still is the domain of young trees and of all kinds of bushes which can exist with little light. At every level there is a different type of vegetation. Likewise the animal species, notably some birds and monkeys, spend practically the whole of their lives at a certain distance from the ground. This is especially true of insects who depend for their food on the flowers of certain species of trees.

Finally on the rain forest floor live the few large species of animals belonging to the forest, and the million-strong army of the 'shadow community'. These are the moulds, bacteria, nematodes, rotiferae, earth worms, spiders, scorpions, centipedes and thousands of species of insects which live for, with and from the other organisms. All of them hold the strange world of the forest in equilibrium and so form a complex chemico-biological ecosystem of unimaginable significance for life on earth.

The tropical forest has a much greater diversity of species

than the woodlands in temperate climatic zones. About 1280 species of plants grow in the Netherlands, 1900 species in Germany and 1500 species in Britain. A tropical rain forest contains about 2000 species of trees alone. The number of plant species is many times greater than this, and the number of animal species is also enormous. There is an almost ineradicable belief that the luxuriant tropical forests only grow on soil that is ideal for agriculture. Nothing is further from the truth. In spite of the unparallelled plant growth, the soil is often poor. This can be because the ground is very old geologically and therefore leached-out, but mostly it is because everything organic is re-absorbed very quickly. That is why anyone who starts to dig into the ground in a luxuriant tropical forest stands a good chance of only finding poor, loosely textured soil.

Through the intense sunlight, the heat and the humidity, the process of photosynthesis goes ahead at full strength. There is a vast production of organic matter, and nowhere else is so much solar energy converted into living material. But there is also a rapid decomposition of dead plants. Under moderate climatic conditions this breakdown goes on gradually, after the dead parts have fallen on to the ground. A layer of humus is then formed, out of which the nutrients are either absorbed by the plant roots or by worms and insects and thus brought back into circulation. In a tropical forest, there is only the barest trace of such a layer of humus, because the heat and humidity cause the breakdown to occur very rapidly. Plants and animals become the food of other plants and animals, either during their life, or directly after their natural death. There are many plants which live independently of the ground; these include the epiphytes – which grow on other plants but do not take nutrients from them – and parasites which do draw on their hosts and neither type needs even the topsoil. When dead leaves and branches fall on the ground, if they are not immediately consumed by a myriad of insects then their remains are absorbed by a fine-meshed network of surface roots.

In spite of this luxuriant growth, there is a shortage of

certain nutrients, which are not manufactured by photo-synthesis, but which are still essential for the development of life, e.g. minerals such as potassium, calcium, phosphorus and magnesium. This is why the vegetation present, in spite of its abundance, contains a comparatively small amount of these nutrients. Consequently, it requires a considerable effort from the larger animals to collect enough salts to keep their bodies in condition. Together with the lack of sunlight, this explains why only a relatively small density of higher animals is found in these forests.

Another reason why these animals need a large area in order to find enough food is that, as a result of there being a large number of different plant families, only a few examples of any single species of tree are found, per hectare. Many animals depend on certain trees for their existence, and so have to travel great distances. This is self-evident for insects which live on honey. But monkeys, too, sometimes have to make long journeys to find the trees which bear the fruit they will eat. As a result, large tracts of primeval forest have to be maintained in order to cater for these species.

The three-toed sloth even exists by the grace mainly of one species of tree, the *Cecropia*. These barely-animate creatures spend long periods of time in one tree hanging upside down. So much so that it has often been suggested that they spend their lives in one tree. They are now known to move more (but not much more) than was once thought: continuation of the species might, otherwise, be a problem.

Source of Inspiration

The primeval forest is a treasury of curiosities and wonders. A small number of gorillas still survives in Africa, and the orang-utan in Indonesia, animals which in many respects are nearly as highly-developed as man. In the coastal rain forest of eastern Brazil there are still a few hundred specimens of the golden lion marmoset, from the family of the smallest monkey in the world. This little creature has an impressive mane and a long tail, but weighs barely a hundred grammes. The story goes, that long ago these little creatures, whose bright gold hair was almost iridescent used to be worn by the Indians in their hair as a living head ornament.

The quetzal still lives on in Central America; an amazing bird with a tail often well over sixty centimetres long. For centuries its existence was only known to science because it appeared in illustrations in the temple ruins of the Mayas and Aztecs. However, what is probably the strangest bird of all lives in Brazil and bears the name of *Opisthocomus hoazin rhehoatzin*. At first sight it looks like a frightened hen, but it has some peculiar features. The young hoatzin has claws on its wings, like the first prehistoric reptile that could fly. However it is not particularly good at flying but clambers up trees using its beak and wing claws with considerable agility and, when it is chased dives into the water and escapes by skimming along and diving repeatedly.

Queen Alexandra lives on still in New Guinea. She is a butterfly, also called Queen Alexandra's Birdwing – the largest species known. The female has a wing span of as much as twenty-eight centimetres and the caterpillar is as thick as a thumb and longer than a hand.

The largest flower that has ever existed blooms in Indonesia. This Rafflesia forms a brick-red calyx with a diameter of about a metre. But anyone searching for the plant which can support such a large flower will be disappointed. He will find nothing but some barely perceptible threads of fungus living parasitically at the foot of a liana. And the lianas are also very remarkable plants. They can grow up to two hundred metres long and thirty centimetres thick.

These are just a few random selections from an in-exhaustible supply of natural wonders. Because of its mystery and inaccessibility to man, and the strange beings which live in it, the primeval forest is well-stocked with subjects for newspaper articles, photos, films, radio and television. Through the development of modern means of communication, this function can continue to be extended without necessarily harming the forest itself.

Disappearing Rain Forest

At present about eight million square kilometres of tropical
virgin forest still remain. Longman and Jenik state that half of
all the living mass on earth is situated in the tropical primeval
forests, although these only cover a relatively small area of the
world. Sadly, this small area is shrinking steadily. Sawing
machines and bulldozers rage everywhere. According to
recent estimates, almost forty per cent of the primeval forest
has already vanished in Latin America and South-east Asia,
more than fifty per cent in Africa, and perhaps sixty per cent
in India, Sri Lanka and Burma. It has been established that in
countries such as the Ivory Coast, Madagascar, the
Philippines and Thailand, three to four thousand hectares of
virgin forest are being destroyed every year. In South-east
Asia, at least one million square kilometres of forest is being
cleared in a piecemeal fashion, used briefly for agriculture and
then abandoned. This is called the 'slash and burn agriculture' or 'shifting cultivation', and in Indonesia is given the
name of 'ladang'. As a result of this, and the commercial
felling, an alarming amount of forest is being lost annually,
i.e. 1255 hectares per hour, or twenty hectares in the minute
you take to read this page. If it goes on at this rate, there will
be no tropical forest left in twenty-five years' time, apart from
a few reserves. It is increasingly obvious that much primeval
forest has fallen into the wrong hands. The tropical rain
forests are being removed from the earth and in a very
disturbing fashion. From Indonesia, where large American
and Japanese firms have timber concessions, about 300,000
cubic metres (m^3) of timber was exported in 1966, and in 1972
exports had risen to 13,671,000 m^3. In 1976, about 17 million
m^3 was exported which is equivalent to losing 28 million m^3 of
wood or between 400,000 and 450,000 hectares of tropical
forest. The largest part of this came from Kalimantan
(formerly known as Borneo). Up to now, a total of 26.8
million hectares of virgin forest in Indonesia have been lost
through felling. It is true that the legislation and the qualify-
ing conditions on which the concessions are granted are

sometimes adequate, but they are seldom complied with. But what can we expect in a country of such an enormous size, where money is depreciating in value every day? The few public servants who have the task of supervising the 'reasonable exploitation' are powerless against the timber firms, and against those of their own countrymen whose only goal is to earn as much as possible and as quickly as possible from the timber.

Drama of the Amazon

The largest primeval forest in the world lies around the Amazon: 350 million hectares of woodland, 20,000 species of plants, many millions of smaller organisms and a total of 70 million cubic metres of wood. A region as large as Europe without Russia, where a quarter of all the fresh water in the world flows down to the ocean through one single enormous river. Here there is an enormous store of genetic material, with which food plants could be strengthened and improved, medicines developed and scientific exploration advanced in so many ways. It is a region with an unequalled influence on the climate of the entire world. It also holds a potential supply of countless products for which future generations of humankind may one day be crying out.

All superlatives fall short in describing this piece of nature. One of the most significant occurrences in the geological history of South America was the uplifting of the long chain of the Andes, on the western side of this continent, which must have started about 70 million years ago. An enormous inland sea came into existence, and dried up over the course of many centuries. The water streamed away towards the eastern side and finally only a system of rivers was left. All these have united in one river, the Amazon. For tens of millions of years after this took place, this region remained almost untouched. If the plans for developing this area go through, it will not be long before this, one of the world's largest wildernesses, is cut into ten pieces by a system of highways. Then it is only a question of time before this network becomes finer.

With the 'reclamation' of the Amazonian forests, the government of Brazil thinks it will be able to deal with its great population problem. But the era of performing technological miracles to solve such problems while ignoring the ecological consequences, is over. The happiness of a country's inhabitants is decided to a large extent by the roles played by politics, economics and good living conditions. All these things are connected. If large environmental works are to be undertaken, deep consideration must be given to the consequences, and that has not happened here.

Goodland and Irwin describe how, in the year 1970, a terrible drought prevailed in the North-east of Brazil, a region where hunger is common even under normal circumstances. President Medici paid the region a visit. On 6th June 1970 he promised, in an emotional speech, to take immediate steps to provide part of the population of the arid North-east with a living in the Amazon region. Ten days later, the 'national programme for integration' (PIN) was drawn up, and the construction of two enormous roads through the Amazon region was announced as the first part of this. One was to run from south to north, while the other, the Trans-Amazon road, was to cut through the entire river basin from east to west. This ambitious plan clearly came about as an impulsive act, without adequately considering the consequences beforehand. But once the plan had been elevated to the status of a national project, nobody dared to challenge any of it. On either side of the roads, a hundred kilometre wide strip has been designated for agricultural land. It is fairly certain however, that attempts to cultivate the land will be doomed to failure, and it will not be the first time in Brazil's history that someone has misjudged nature. In 1927, Henry Ford tried to transform a million hectares into rubber plantations. Within ten years, it was a fiasco, as the soil proved to be unsuitable for use as cultivated land.

Many of the other arguments which are advanced in favour of the overhasty construction of the roads are also spurious.

As an aid in checking the results of the population explosion, road building hardly plays a part. There is no military advantage, and it remains to be seen whether the roads are in a favourable situation for the exploitation of minerals. But the technical feasibility is also at issue now. It looks as if the first section of one of these new roads is already overgrown by jungle before the last section is completed. Every country has the obvious right to use its own ground to increase its prosperity, but the right to mismanagement is given to no-one. No prosperity comes about if nature is misunderstood and destroyed. No civilization can take root in a waste land.

Nature conservationists often use the blackmail argument: 'If you violate and destroy nature, then the whole world will be annihilated.' If this argument is listened to, it is rarely understood. Those contractors who exploit the timber tend to see only their own direct interest. The government which grants a timber concession wants to see yields in the shortest term possible. The most common understanding people have of the connection between conservation of the primeval forest, where modern human never set foot, and the future development of their own nation, is that the forests stand in the way of the development. And so, the axe is in.

People need to sort everything out clearly before they can absorb it. This is because of the human inability to think in long units of time. People think in space, not in time. We are good at calculating distances and co-ordinating the movement between two points but when it comes to applying these same patterns of thought to time, it proves impossible for many people. Not very many people plan for more than a few years ahead, if that much. And, similarly, experiences of the past are, so often, quickly forgotten.

This small fact has great consequences. One who is unable to think in terms of time is unlikely to understand processes which require a great deal of time during which they may change dynamically. Modern social sciences, such as sociology and economics, suffer strikingly from this fault: they make 'snapshots' of concepts and happenings which are continually changing with time so that the view is of something superficial and temporary. Economics has never paid much attention to nature, presumably because nature is a dynamic system with very many 'delays'. Changes are slow. 'Sapling great, planter dead' says the old adage, suggesting that there is not much point in planting the tree, because it takes so long before it yields anything.

It is seldom possible to give people a complete understanding of nature. Only when the problem has been split up into parts does an understanding begin to dawn. This can be done by separating the various qualities of nature from one another, and looking at each one individually.

The forest, for example, has many functions or possible uses, which can be described and evaluated independently of each other. Understandably though, such a division fails to show the true significance of it as a whole, because these functions often overlap or are interdependent. They are summarised at the end of this chapter in a list whose sequence is based on a rather unusual division. Woodlands are generally classified according to the species of trees which are most commonly found there (i.e. the dominant species). This variation according to species is connected with the climate and the nature of the soil amongst other things. Here we are trying out another method: we classify the woodlands according to the extent to which they can be regarded as 'wild' or 'natural', and we speak of primary, secondary or artificial woodlands.

In an old, climax forest the many changes that occur (growing, germinating, dying off, etc.), more or less neutralize one another. Large tracts of such forest will not naturally disappear or downgrade in quality or diversity. The greater the diversity of the forest, the stronger this state of equilibrium will be. How great that diversity becomes will depend on climate and soil, but the maximum number that any site can support at a particular time is nearly always present. This type of vegetation, left undisturbed for centuries, and hardly changing any more, is called *primary*. Virgin forests, of which the tropical forest is one of the most important forms, can be called 'primary forests'. A virgin forest loses its primary character when people begin to interfere with it.

So long as human infiltration into the forest is limited to a small number of scattered inhabitants, such as pygmies, Indians, and an occasional scientific expedition searching for new species or wishing to be of service to culture, the character of the primeval forest will not change appreciably. However, the situation is quite different if the people start building settlements, hunting over wider areas or taking out the best trees for their wood. The result of the disturbance is that the vegetation acquires another character. That the equilibrium is broken is obvious from the fact that all kinds of higher animal species take flight and disappear. The outcome of this kind of interference, of the original forest disappearing and new woods growing up spontaneously in its place, is that a type of woodland develops which we call *secondary*. When, for example, the most desirable kinds of wood are felled out of a virgin forest – and these are often the largest and oldest trees – one finds, not very surprisingly, that the plants and animals whose existence depends on the presence of these trees also disappear. Furthermore, sun and rain are suddenly able to reach spots which used to be inaccessible. So 'wild shoots' spring up to form what is called 'secondary vegetation'. This is totally different, in its wealth of interdependent species and manner of growth, from what had stood there before.

In a primeval forest dominant trees live long, grow slowly and take plenty of time for their reproduction. Their seeds need not be scattered over a wide area and in any case receive a large food reserve, because they have to germinate in a shady environment.

With the secondary growth, which germinates in open terrain, the situation is quite different. In order to start growing, the young plants have to strike root as soon as possible. These pioneers grow rapidly in their youth and quickly produce a large number of seeds, which are scattered over a great area by many means. Theoretically, an old, 'primary' forest ought to be able to grow out of such a young secondary forest. If we are concerned about the disappearance of the primary rain forest, it is because the transition from secondary to primary forest takes so long: thousands to tens of thousands of years. The 'delay' in this system is too great, as the shifting cultivation obligingly demonstrates. In times when the sprinkling of inhabitants of the primeval forest still practised 'ladang' cultivation, they slashed small areas of the forest and burned them down so that they could practise agriculture there for a few years. Such a small clearing could soon grow over again and be swallowed up by the forest in the course of time. Yet the research worker, Dr. J. P. Schulz, who has made a study of the primeval forest in Surinam, has recorded a difference in the growth, caused by Indians who must have lived there many centuries ago! Their presence was proved by the find of some pieces of earthenware in the soil.

In the primeval forest on the Table Mountain in New Guinea an observant forester has noted something similar. The wood looked like an original tropical rain forest, but when he analysed the species of trees, he found a shortage of certain species in the upper storey. At first he thought that it was an accidental deviation, but when a water pipe was being laid in the ground, remains were found from a people of the Bronze Age.

Many primeval forests have been lost through felling, fire and erosion and, in some places, new woodlands of secondary vegetation have grown up. In most Western countries there is no virgin forest.

Our third forest type is the *artificial* woodland. This is planted by man and for a variety of reasons. For example, a forest can help to stabilize shifting desert sand. In olden days, lovers of the chase had many forests planted in which to pursue their sport. Timber production is also a well-known incentive. Today, the recreation function of woodlands is valued so highly that this is a fresh inducement to start planting them. The still fairly young woods, which are planted for one purpose or another, are called artificial woodlands.

In the table, the various functions of forests are examined

one by one, with a view to finding out which is the *main* type
of forest performing them:

FUNCTIONS OF THE FOREST AND THE MAIN FOREST TYPE
WHICH PERFORMS THE FUNCTION.

1 *Reserve function*
Guarantee of potential benefits which are still   Primary
unknown. The preservation of functions
which are still unknown or not yet understood.

2 *Source of life*
Trapping solar energy in living cells. The   Primary
gradual or abrupt creation of new living
organisms (evolution).

3 *Improved breeds*
The supply of genetic stock for breeds in   Primary
commercial timber production, arable
farming, horticulture and stockbreeding, or
the improvement of existing breeds by cross-
breeding.

4 *Science*
Source of new discoveries in many branches   Primary
of science. Materials and workplace for study
and investigation.

5 *Culture*
Inspiration for art and culture. Subjects for   Primary
verbal and visual information supplied for   Secondary
education and relaxation (films, books, etc.)

6 *Vegetable products*
Storehouse of fibres, medicinal plants, spices,   Primary
resin oils, fruit, honey and so forth.   Secondary

7 *Animal products*
Supply of protein, horn, skins, wool and other   Primary
products of wild animals (by means of limited   Secondary
hunting and trapping).

8 *Wood*
Source of energy (fuel). Raw material for
structures, paper and countless other
purposes.

Primary
Secondary
Artificial

9 *Climate*
Influence on the climate, both globally and
locally. Prevention of natural disasters.

Primary
Secondary
Artificial

10 *Topsoil*
Preservation of fertile soil. Humus formation.
Prevention of erosion.

Secondary
Artificial

11 *Purification*
Disposal of waste matter in soil and water.
Trapping of toxic substances. Trapping dust
from the air.

Primary
Secondary
Artificial

12 *Water regulation*
Regulation of the water cycles. Gradual
release of rain water for streams and rivers,
irrigation, power stations and shipping.

Primary
Secondary
Artificial

13 *Tourism*
Source of wonder and place to visit for tourist
traffic and holiday makers.

Primary
Secondary
Artificial

14 *Landscape*
Embellishment of the landscape (sometimes
as an element of *deliberate* landscaping).

Secondary
Artificial

15 *Health*
Aid to promotion and restoration of physical
condition – as a place for exercising, camping,
etc.

Artificial

16 *Recreation*
Relaxation in the direct vicinity of home and
place of work.

Artificial

The Reserve Function

The table shows how obviously important the 'wild' forest really is. A great many of the most comprehensive functions are performed by the primary forest. The first, the reserve function, is the most important, but also the least known. Dr. M. Jacobs, a biologist of the Rijksherbarium (the Dutch State Herbarium) in Leiden, calls this function 'respect for creation or, if one likes, for evolution'. 'Nature' he writes, 'means that which is born. Some humility and solicitude seem to be fitting with regard to that which came into existence without any help at all from us. The question of renewal confronts us with the limits of technological power; power which will only remain so by well-taught application'. It follows from this opinion that anyone who wants to keep the natural world in good condition must use it as a standard for his own ambitions; compared with nature his own technical achievement will shrink into insignificance.

But the reserve function is more than this. Species of plants and animals die out without any apparent cause. Sometimes we find out the reason – e.g. there may be a concentration of toxin in the food chain of the animal, which is fatal in the last link, where it accumulates. This is a simple case. Other cases appear less simple. Too many individuals of a species can cause its end, and clearly, so can too few. But plants and animals have only one goal – the preservation of the species. There is no reason to assume that this is not the case, or close to it, in humans – although many ingenious arguments have been devized in opposition to the idea. This instinct for the preservation of the species dominates social and cultural life. The willingness for example to set aside part of one's income for the payment of insurance premiums is probably prompted by it. Premiums are paid against illness, death and accidents, even when people don't anticipate any of these disasters.

Preservation of the virgin forests as 'reserve' areas is identical. It is a premium against possible uncertainties in the future, and for humans, this cannot be considered unnatural. It is, therefore, more remarkable that their behaviour is so little in keeping with this principle.

Nine. The Great Store-Room

'There is no such thing as mankind going on without wildlife . . . If you lose your genetic diversity, you are out of the business of high yield agriculture permanently.'
Paul Ehrlich. 1973

Nature as a source of new breeds

Essentially, this function involves supplying genetic material for improvement of breeds used in arable farming, horticulture, stockbreeding and forestry, and is based on the fact that inherited characteristics exist in nature and are stored. These inherited characteristics are transmitted from generation to generation by 'genes'. Genes are codings within the cells, made up of strings of DNA (Deoxyribose Nucleic Acid) each of which has a different and specific structure. Every gene is the bearer of certain characteristics. In reproduction the genes are divided between the offspring in a fixed proportion. In stockbreeding and arable farming it is most important that the breeds used possess certain lasting characteristics, e.g. the ability to produce many offspring, to grow rapidly, or to show resistance to diseases and pests. Sometimes it is possible to cultivate breeds of plants or animals in which the same desired genes recur in the same combination. This makes a breed consistent and productive and, thus, economically important. These characteristics can be lost over a long period and attempts must be made to retrieve them by cross-breeding with other stocks.

The food of millions of people depends on whether we can continually improve our most important agricultural crops in this manner. All farm animals and cultivated plants originate from wild species. Originally these species were used in the form in which they occur in nature and, as time has passed, they have been made gradually more suitable for arable farming and cattle breeding and so forth. Some people think that it is no longer necessary to use wild species because the process of improvement is complete. In fact, the process is scarcely under way, and conditions which require new breeds are continually arising.

For instance, when we want to increase the agricultural production in the developing countries, breeds must be found which are adapted to the local conditions. Then it may be necessary to breed back from the distant ancestors of the present varieties or to look for completely new species, still growing wild in those countries.

As an example, it is a problem that breeds of cattle, pigs, sheep and poultry which have, over many generations, become completely adapted to the moderate climate of Europe and North America, show little or no resistance to many diseases in hot countries. They are also not accustomed to the kind of feed-stuffs they are given there. Consequently new varieties have to be bred, and wild species which are native to these hot countries, having evolved in that climate and with that vegetation for thousands of years, are obviously ideal for the purpose.

The difficulties caused in over-populated countries by environmental pollution can also result in a need for crops with new characteristics. If a farmer wants to make less use of toxic chemical sprays in pest control, he must search for breeds that will resist the diseases which, until then, were combated by those chemicals. Resistance to disease is one of the most important characteristics that selective breeding tries to achieve. The various diseases regularly occur in the regions where the wild ancestors of the modern crops grow. In nature, we have explained that a certain equilibrium has come about between disease-producing bacteria, viruses and moulds on the one hand and the plant on the other. The plant has developed some resistance to these pressures, so it is logical to call on nature's gene pool to help solve the problems caused by nature.

This is not so simple as it may sound. Expeditions have to collect the wild plants and their useful characteristics must be investigated with endless patience to see how best they can serve in breeding agricultural crops. Here is another field for research in which comparatively little has been done. The possibilities seem to be inexhaustible.

Scientists working on the cultivation of crops, and organisations concerned with food supply, such as the FAO and UNESCO, are very worried at the loss of much useful material with the depletion of wilderness areas. This concerns not only the ancestors of our present agricultural strains but, perhaps more particularly, those plants which will be eradicated even before their properties are known – species which may be as valuable as the fungus penicillin has been.

In addition, many varieties used in primitive agriculture since time immemorial may disappear as a result of the increasing use of modern large-scale methods and the strains which belong to them.

Because collecting wild plants is such a tremendous task, people have looked for other methods of preserving them. At the moment there are two possibilities. The first is to make collections of plants which have to grow and flower afresh every year in order to keep them available. This is rather laborious. The other, rather easier system, is to store the seed; but this is not possible for all species, and it is also an arduous and complicated business. This is clear from the collection of the Russian research worker Vavilov, who went on more than two hundred expeditions, in Russia and abroad, between 1920 and 1940 and finally had a seed collection in his institute containing more than 250,000 examples. Unfortunately, Vavilov fell into disgrace in Russia and a large part of his collection was lost after his death. After the Second World War, the remains were divided between several institutes.

Such large seed collections, managed by specialist scientists, are called 'gene banks'. The largest, with 500,000 examples, is in Colorado, U.S.A. However, one of the difficulties is that the viability of seeds is often limited. This can vary from less than one year to several centuries. Tropical plants are notable among those whose seeds can, as a rule, only be kept for a short time. Another difficulty is that inherited characteristics of the plant species in the gene banks are not always constant, because of the influence of varying climatic conditions and abrupt genetic changes (mutations). So, while the gene banks may be very useful they do not offer a substitute for nature.

Many of the ancestors of crop plants inhabit wilderness areas in high mountainous regions, with much sun. An enormous variety of uncommon plant species grows there. Perhaps this is caused by the high concentration of ultra-violet rays which seems to stimulate the development of new species. All kinds of biological, soil and climatic conditions may be present, through which the wealth of species increases. Vavilov was the first to point out this remarkable accumulation of different plant species and indicated a number of regions where many of the crop plants originated.

Next to agriculture, medicine has gained the most from nature. It is estimated that $20-30\%$ of all medicines are at present derived, in one way or another, from nature. A good example is acetyl salicylic acid, commonly known as 'aspirin'; the acid was isolated from willow bark by a German doctor in 1899. Illnesses which used to be fatal are now fought with antibiotics which were also discovered in nature not very long ago. They are derived from moulds, of which it is estimated that some hundreds of thousands of, largely unknown, species still exist in nature – chiefly in forest soils.

The economic value of this function of nature cannot be estimated in money. Benefits which only become available in the very long term never fit into the economic calculations commonly used now. But even without such a calculation, the maintenance of gene pools has an obvious significance for the present or a future economy.

THE POTATO

An important example of the relationship between nature and

The change of primary into secondary forest

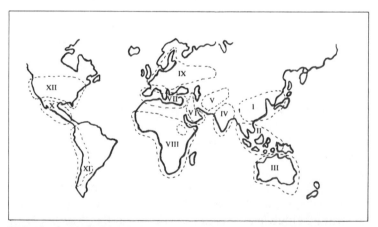

Macro-centres of crop plants according to Vavilov and Zukovsky I China and Japan. II Indonesia and Indo-China. III Australia. IV India. V Central Asia. VI Near East. VII Mediterranean area. VIII Africa with Ethopia. IX Europe with Siberia. X Central America. XI South America. XII North America.

cultivated crops is the common potato. Four hundred years ago, the potato was a virtually unknown plant from South America. Only two hundred years ago, Louis XVI of France wanted to make it a food for the people, but his subjects had no desire to eat this animal feed-stuff. They thought it was poisonous. So the king had the 'Royal Potato Fields' laid, outside Paris, and guarded by soldiers. These potatoes were destined for the king's table exclusively. At night hungry thieves stole potatoes from the fields, and the soldiers had orders to see and hear nothing. Soon the potato became a generally accepted food among the people.

However, it is very susceptible to disease and only thrives in a few parts of the world. Consequently, growers are doing their utmost to breed varieties which are disease-resistant, so eliminating the need for pesticides. A search is also being made for varieties that grow well under different climatic conditions, so that the potato may become available for more countries than at present. Between 1925 and 1966, no fewer than twenty-four expeditions set out to collect wild species of potato and the research is still going on. In some countries, such as Paraguay, no search was made for wild species of potato until recently. Now 150 wild species have been identified in South America. Only about seven of these have been cultivated.

WHEAT

Unlike most other crop plants, it is likely that nearly all the wild species of wheat are known. That does not mean that they are all available in collections and gene banks. There are so many wild varieties that all the possibilities they offer have not yet been tested.

In Israel a great many different varieties have been collected, and extensively used by European growers in developing strains which are resistant to the so-called 'yellow rust'.

The more primitive species of wheat have been vanishing from use even among the small-scale farmers. For example, a species called 'spelt', which gives flour of very good quality has practically disappeared from the upland plains of Persia, where it was a much-cultivated crop for a very long time. For the development of strong strains in the future, we shall have to depend far more on species found in the wild.

RICE

The position with rice is very similar. Until a short time ago, twenty wild species were known, only two of which were cultivated. Here, too, new agricultural methods have now caused many old strains to disappear. New strains give a higher yield but are very vulnerable. The International Institute for Rice Research, which was founded in 1962, has collected about 900 wild strains in recent years and created a pool of crop plants which have vanished from other places, so as to build up a safety buffer against diseases, pests and degeneration of the most productive kinds.

FRUIT

The Middle East is traditionally a region where all kinds of fruit originated. Until a short time ago, very little had been done to complete a record of the wealth of genetic material present there. Unfortunately, it is probably too late already. Some thirty years ago the Turkish government set up highly mechanized nurseries, which have developed so quickly that they now supply about 80% of all the young fruit trees in the country. While taking a short-term view, this appears to be a favourable practice for the prosperity of the country, over a longer term it may threaten many wild and semi-domesticated species with extinction.

FENUGREEK

In former centuries, fenugreek (from the fenugreek plant) was a popular cough medicine (and an effective one), a remedy against piles and a love potion. Ground fenugreek is an indispensible ingredient of curry. On Halmaheira, a drink was brewed from fenugreek which was supposed to prevent pregnancy, and it seems that the inhabitants of this island were on to something, for it may become a source of raw materials for the contraceptive pill. The pill contains some hormones made chiefly from diosgenine, a substance found mainly in one particular wild plant in Mexico, and which will only grow wild. Because the production of diosgenine is quite a hazardous affair – with having to collect the wild-growing plants – the fenugreek plant may offer a solution. Diosgenine is present in its seeds and, as a bonus, it appears that it can be cultivated.

COFFEE

Whether coffee is a food-plant or a remedy is a question for debate. There is, in any case, a great variety of coffee plants found in nature. How important it is to preserve this store was shown in the spring of 1975 when French investigators found, on the Comoro Islands (between Malagasy and East Africa), a wild coffee plant which did not contain a single trace of caffeine! A historic discovery, which will undoubtedly lead to enormous sales in due course. How can we assess the true economic value of nature's gene pool when the discovery of just one species can result in a turnover in world trade?

WATER PLANTS

An example which will appeal strongly to technologists is the power which some water plants have of purifying water more efficiently and cheaply than a man-made plant can. A water hyacinth found in Florida can extract the very toxic heavy metals from the water – a task which is quite beyond present day technology. Thus it is capable, to a large extent, of purifying industrial effluent. Together with a certain species of rush it is able to purify the water of phosphates and nitrogen compounds, which are so difficult to remove by technical means. It appears that when rushes are used in large numbers they can do the job more efficiently than a man-made purification plant. Furthermore, the costs of constructing a combined rushes/water hyacinth installation are about a sixth, and running costs about a quarter, of those of technical purification. As much as 98% of the water is purified – an impressive achievement. Just how the plants do all this is still not clear. Apparently, the rushes increase the self-purifying capacity of the water, and the water hyacinths concentrate the heavy metals in some obscure way. They would have to be harvested and the metals processed.

Again and again, natural phenomena comparable to human technological achievements are being discovered. It is not likely that an end will come to this for a long time, because only the 'first racks' of nature's 'store-room' have been drawn on.

POPLARS

The poplars of the temperate zones grow quickly, and their wood is suitable for all kinds of purposes. The trees can be cultivated asexually by cuttings so that a great many offspring can be obtained from one tree, all with the same inherited characteristics. This has great advantages in cultivation. Through hybridization people try to obtain varieties which have certain desirable characteristics, then reproduce them further by taking cuttings. There is a continual search for new varieties. Poplar species have been found at great heights in Kenya and the Himalayas where there is a long growing season. In the far north, on the other hand, there are species which have to make the most of a short season and therefore characteristically come into leaf very quickly in spring. The trick is producing a breed through hybridization, which comes into leaf quickly but keeps on growing until the end of a long summer. Whilst improving the poplar, most attention has been paid, so far, to rapid growth and fine, straight trunks. Now, however, just as much interest is being shown in characteristics which still occur in existing varieties. These days, landscape planning is given increasing importance particularly in urbanized areas. This has created a demand for trees which look picturesque, grow quickly, are resistant to sea-wind and, if possible, can also supply useful wood. Because of this, landscapers have become interested in the black poplar, a native tree, of which large numbers were once found in the Netherlands and Southern England, in the extensive forests along their rivers. In the 18th and 19th centuries it was still widely planted in parks and beside lakes, as illustrated in the landscape paintings of Constable. In those days, more male trees were planted than female. The male is more attractive because of its beautiful red catkins which dangle from the branches like plumes. The female trees have the disadvantage that they produce large quantities of fluff in summer, which was unpopular with fruit growers because it stuck to the ripe fruit and made it unsaleable. Fewer female trees were grown and this discrimination was one of the main reasons for cross-pollination often being impossible – especially when the number of male trees decreased as well.

In the maritime climate the black poplar has evolved with a resistance to sea-wind. By hybridization with species which still grow wild, it is now possible to cultivate varieties which grow quickly in the coastal provinces, in spite of the strong wind, and furnish good wood. With the help of this species it is also possible now to bring more variety into plantations. This is urgently needed in the Netherlands and Britain because some of the familiar trees such as the elm and the hawthorn, which were once the bringers of green and shade to the countryside, are falling victim to Dutch elm disease and bacterial pests. To a certain extent the black poplar can take their place in England and the World Wildlife Fund has instigated a search for the black poplar. In the Netherlands too, after an extensive search, wild species have been found which possess the desired hereditary characteristics.

The economic value of all this genetic 'reserve', expressed in monetary terms, is difficult, if not impossible, to estimate. Yet every gain which is made from these properties of nature is of economic advantage, because it satisfies human needs. When the last remains of nature have been swept away, all this will no longer be possible.

Ten. A Horn of Plenty

*De toutes les branches de l'Economie, la plus
vitale pour l'avenir de l'homme, pour son
bien-être et même pour sa survie est
l'Economie de la Nature, c'est-à-dire
l'organisation de la production et de la
consommation des richesses immatérielles
nées du milieu naturel.*
            Philippe Saint Marc.

The many functions of woodland

With remarkable persistence, nature conservationists are
constantly calling attention to human dependence on plants
and animals. With equal persistence, the exploiters and
destroyers of nature remain incredulous. But there is hope yet
of a break-through in communications and just a little
understanding may be possible. If we describe nature in
terms of commercial abundance, then we can argue the case
for conservation in economic terms.

There is not much point in going into a description of the
daily activities of an average westerner, whose petrol was
derived from plants, whose shirt comes from petroleum and
plants, and whose house is heated by natural gas which is also
derived from plants. The reaction to this is that prehistoric
nature has nothing to do with the natural environment we
have now, and that modern humans passed the stage of direct
dependence on nature long ago. The latter is simply not true
however, and it is easy to forget that 'modern man' also exists
in non-western countries. There are 3,000 million people in
the Third World countries mostly living far closer to nature
than those in the 'developed' countries, and therefore far
more dependent on it. The prolific discussion about the world
energy crisis pays scant regard to these people, many of whom

have never heard of oil, natural gas or coal, and whose main source of energy is coppice-wood, dry sticks and dried cow-dung. 'The other energy crisis' is how Erik Eckholm of the Worldwatch Institute describes the state of distress in which three quarters of mankind will find itself if the trees and forests disappear. Not only does a great energy source thus disappear, but also a source of food and all kinds of other resources. In large parts of the world, the rural cultures still have a fortuitous and dependent relationship with nature. It is not very sophisticated, and nature often offers her services in an arbitrary form. But millions of people still exist from day to day on what is provided by streams, woodland and thickets, with perhaps a little primitive agriculture.

SUPPLY OF TIMBER

The world is crying out for wood. Some think of wood perhaps only in planks, broom-handles and window-frames. But there is a great quantity of wood used without most people being aware of it. Good observers may recognise wood as a raw material in chipboard, fibreboard, paper and card-board, which are used in very large quantities. Wood is also an enormous source of energy through the heat it gives out when burnt. Lastly, it is an indispensable raw material for so many products whose origins few people realize.

Of all the functions of forests, 'supplier of wood' is that which can most easily be expressed in monetary terms. It presents no problems for economists and would not need to be dealt with here if it were not widely held that the world no longer has any great need for wood.

Before too long there will be an almost universal shortage of wood. According to the FAO, the Common Market countries will be short of nearly 170 million m³ of wood in 1980. This is equivalent to the production on 50 to 60 million hectares of woodland, whereas there are only 27 million hectares in the Common Market now.

It is also alarming that the northern European countries – which are traditionally famous for their timber production – are themselves beginning to experience a shortage. Finland, which until recently had the largest net export of wood for the manufacture of fibreboard and stationery, is now forced to import wood to keep its own wood-working industry going. Its own forests can no longer maintain the supply. Even Sweden will be short of wood in 1980. Norway already has to import 2.5 million m^3 of round timber annually, while its export of wood pulp is barely covered by the import of wood for paper and board. Being so very densely populated and industrial, Japan badly needs timber. For its population China, too, has only a small amount of wood. These countries obtain much of their wood supply from the Asian part of Russia. Here there is still some potential for further timber production, but the forests grow very slowly in these regions, and the vast distances present an almost insuperable problem. Export of timber from the Soviet Union in any case, is more likely to decrease than increase, because of the growing domestic need.

Moreover, the need for wood, per head of the world population, will probably rise sharply. The director of the Stichting Industrie-Hout in the Netherlands (Foundation for Industrial Woods), Mr. H. A. van der Meiden, has tried to work out how much additional wood would be needed if the relative consumption in other prosperous areas of the world was as great as that in the United States. With the population at its present level, 5,500 million m^3 of wood would be needed, outside the United States, to make up the difference. A rise of more than six times the present production rate would be required. A similar calculation, applied to the developing countries in Africa, South America and Asia (but excluding Japan and Russia), indicates that raising the relative consumption level to that of the United States would make it necessary to produce twenty-five times as much timber in those countries. Understandably, the United States uses a lot of wood. It would be admirable enough if these countries would envisage their timber consumption per head rise only to the level of the Common Market. In that case the output would not have to be multiplied by twenty-five but by ten. It hardly helps to reduce the problem.

A SOURCE OF ENERGY

Every tree and every bush is a collector of solar energy. To give an impression of the amount of solar energy which is converted in a forest into the most accessible form, namely wood, the following comparison may be helpful.

In 1967, world timber production averaged 2,100 million m³, which is an economic production of about £23,000 million, worth about £11 per cubic metre. As it is barely possible to work out an average the figure is arbitrary. For there are thousands of species of trees over the world, with countless local and international possibilities for exploitation. In 1976 this timber production had almost doubled, so that more than £44,000 million worth of trees were cut down and carpentered or pulverized for paper and other products. Imagine that in 1967 the total number of trees felled was not quite large enough to affect the total world stocks of trees permanently. In other words, at that time the number of trees felled equalled the natural growth of the forest. Assuming this, the yield for the year 1967 would be equivalent to the maximum interest which, on the basis of the timber production alone, can be accrued from the forest capital. With a five per cent rate of interest, that capital would then have been about £440,000 million. Because forests also have countless other functions, which, incidentally, do not reduce the potential timber production, their value has to be added to that of the timber produced. How gigantic this capital is, and how important it could be if managed responsibly, may be indicated by the following, theoretical, example: an electric power station of 1000 Megawatt (a very large station) situated in a forest and stoked by wood, could operate at full strength, year in year out, if the following conditions were complied with:

1 It must stand in the centre of a forest region with a radius of eighteen kilometres, with an average haulage distance for the timber of twelve kilometres.

2 The irradiation conversion on efficiency is 1% (i.e. 1% of the solar energy is converted into wood).
3 The volume of new timber growth each year is equivalent to the total amount felled.

In wooded countries, there is a great deal to gain by using the natural conversion of solar energy for urgently needed energy production. One minor advantage is that the technique for this kind of production is simple, compared with nuclear fission, for example, or direct solar energy conversion, the technology of which is still in its infancy.

This tempting prospect has some drawbacks, of course. Intensive utilization of the natural wood growth will cause intolerable interference for many plant and animal species. Timber production would take priority over wildlife conservation. Also, the effect of returning to the environment the water that has been used in a cooling system ought to be taken into account, because it raises the temperature of the natural water, often to the detriment of the life in it. Then there is the problem of energy transmission. Such power stations are not sited in places where the demand for energy is greatest. There are solutions to this – for example, by converting the energy which has been generated into hydrogen, which can be transported – but the question of practicability is in itself not very important. The point is that this example gives some idea of the enormous potential of nature for a techno-economic culture. That is – a forest with a radius of eighteen kilometres can provide the material for an energy flow of 1,000 Megawatts. Reduce this into oil and gas consumption and apply the figures to the Amazon region. The results will be impressive.

OXYGEN SUPPLY AND AIR PURIFICATION

A well-used argument for conserving the forests and seas of the world is the key role they play in supplying our oxygen. If we want to go on breathing we have to preserve the primeval forests many conservationists say, when no other argument is persuasive enough. And this is an interesting way of emphasising the economic significance of nature. Calculate the amount of oxygen produced per hectare of woodland; relate it to the cost of producing oxygen artificially; and you have a ready-made argument for putting great economic pressure on the wood-chopping inhabitants of tropical countries. Conversely, those inhabitants also have a fine political weapon in their hands: give us what we want, or we'll turn off the oxygen. But the world's oxygen cannot be produced in the same way other commodities are produced. The element of oxygen does not increase in quantity because of the existence of forests. So the oxygen production of forests and seas is not important in this sense.

This seems very strange given that photosynthesis, which takes place in green plants, is the only natural process by which oxygen is liberated. In this reaction, solar energy is used to combine water with carbon dioxide to produce several kinds of carbon compounds, such as wood, starch and sugars, and oxygen is released into the air or is absorbed by water. But anything built up in this way is always broken down again, because all these natural processes are just parts of cycles. All the carbon compounds produced will eventually cease to be compounds, during plant respiration, for example, and later when the plant dies and decomposes in the soil. Through these processes *the oxygen released is used again* and carbon dioxide is liberated. In this case there is one cycle for carbon and another for oxygen. No net increase in oxygen is produced to be used freely elsewhere. Consequently trees and plants do not have a service production function because, in the end, they always re-use what they first produce. Only when organic material *disappears* from this cycle is there a surplus of oxygen, although it is only temporary. This happens naturally when plants are preserved without decaying; plankton, for example, might sink to the bottom of the sea and be trapped by layers of ooze, or a marsh become overgrown with sphagnum or bog moss, and peat, coal, oil and gas are formed. When these minerals are burned they use up their share in the oxygen cycle and it is completed. But not altogether, because thirty-two grammes of oxygen are required for the combustion of every twelve grammes of bound, or free, carbon. If all the woodlands on earth were cut down and burned, something would obviously be lost. Calculating from the above proportion, the loss would amount to less than 0·001% of the world's oxygen supply.

Clearly there is no world shortage of oxygen, but regional deficiencies can occur. The pleasant experience of the city dweller who takes a deep breath of fresh air in a wood or park is apparently explained by the lack of something in the city. But the refreshment is more likely to be the result of the trees' air-purifying effect than of their oxygen production.

Let us consider one single tree for a change. A hundred year old beech tree has some hundreds of thousands of leaves. A German research worker, Bernatsky, counted as many of 800,000. With that number, the total apparent surface area of the leaves is 1600 square metres. The leaves possess millions of stomata – holes through which the carbon dioxide in the air penetrates into the leaf cell. Because of these openings, the surface area of the leaf is increased about a hundredfold, and is thus about 160,000 square metres. This enormous surface is one vast chemical factory, which plays an indispensable part in the carbon and oxygen cycles every day. If the beech weighs 2,500 kilos then during its lifetime it will have removed the carbon dioxide from over 12.5 million m³ of air. In one hour, this tree converts 2,350 grammes of carbon dioxide and 960 grammes of water into 1,600 grammes of sugars (glucose), while liberating 1,712 grammes of oxygen, and using more than 6,000 calories (25,080 joules) of sunlight.

These 1,600 square metres of beech leaves absorb 320,000 calories (1,337,600 joules) per hour from sunlight, while only 6,000 are used for its own glucose production. The remainder is reflected back and is mainly used in the evaporation of water. As the tree respires (breathes) it burns up some of the sugars produced, using oxygen in the process and, unlike the procedure in photosynthesis, oxygen is used and carbon dioxide is liberated. The relationship between the oxygen production and its consumption in respiration is, however, always such that only between one third and one fifth of the total consumed is re-used. The rest is used for growth, the production of biomass, the vegetative material which makes animal (including human) life possible.

The foliage cover of trees and plants performs an important function by intercepting dust. In the German Ruhr area alone one million tons of dust are spewed out each year. In New York, three tons are deposited per hectare every year, and in London, one ton per hectare every year. Very fine dust is not deposited in the lungs but is exhaled again. Coarser dust is absorbed by the mucus membrane in the throat and nose. Medium sized dust does, however, remain in the body, where it can cause illness. The large beech tree, with its leaf area of 1,600 square metres, intercepts several hundred kilos of this dust, filtering it out of the air. When there is a shower of rain, the dust is washed off the leaves to become part of the soil. A hectare of fir wood retains thirty-two tons of dirt from the air, a hectare of pine trees thirty-five tons, and a hectare of beechwood sixty-five tons. That is, until it rains, after which a fresh supply of atmospheric pollutants can be retained.

Deciduous trees are naturally the most efficient in performing the dust-filtering function – especially the alder, willow, oak, plane and beech, which have a great resistance to atmospheric pollution and so can grow well in regions where their air-purifying effect is most needed. Anyone who walks in an avenue of trees, or a park, therefore breathes filtered air, which is also cooler because the trees provide shade and reflect the irradiated heat of the sun and any surrounding buildings.

In 1971, two 'purification towers' about the size of advertisement pillars were erected in the Avenue de Ledru-Rollin in Paris. They cost 27,500 French francs at the time but, when mass-produced, the price fell to 8000 French francs. The capacity is 100 million cubic metres of air, containing 0.3 to one milligramme of dust per cubic metre. So one tower can extract thirty to fifty kilos of dust from the air annually, and several thousand of them would be needed to extract the dust from the Parisian air. Not unnaturally the towers are operated by electricity, the generation of which, of course, creates pollution elsewhere. Trees however, are more efficient, do not create pollution elsewhere, and work for nothing into the bargain. They are also more aesthetically satisfying.

Summing up: the influence of woodlands on the world's supply of oxygen, except in the extremely long term, is very low, bearing in mind the almost closed cycle of carbon and oxygen, and the fact that the available oxygen supply is approximately five million times as great as the total daily release of oxygen from all the trees in the world. Where a lot of oxygen is used a local shortage may occur if the new supply falls short for one reason or another. When the air is heated and polluted, it is usually not the trees' oxygen production but their air purifying and cooling effect which tends to improve the atmosphere.

One can start to estimate the economic value of this purifying function of trees by asking what would be needed if they could no longer fulfil the function. As it is not possible to construct a substitute machine which does not produce at least as much pollution as it removes, this 'compensation' hypothesis has to be tested on a natural substitute. So the only alternative is more trees. The replacement of a tree by other trees and the costs involved give a rough indication of its immediate value. Since it is only possible to use young trees as a replacement, we cannot substitute a sapling for that single one hundred year old tree and then wait a hundred years. We require 1700 young beech trees, with a crown diameter of one metre, to do the same work as that one solitary hundred year old tree. In 1979 it would cost about £8000 ($16000) to acquire and plant those 1700 trees.

TREES MAKE THE LANDSCAPE

The new specialist field of landscape architecture has only recently come into existence and trees and shrubs play an important part in it, often having to cover up the careless damage caused by man with his roads and buildings. But what exactly is the landscape? Even landscape architects find it rather difficult to define. It may be simplest to say that it is everything which we experience with our senses when we are outside an urban area. On the whole, this is what we see, but when we are in the open air it is also the things we smell and hear. Where the latter is concerned, this is really a negative merit. Already it is a strange sensation for many people to be in a place where silence exists – with at most the rustling of leaves or the sounds made by wild animals. Usually the landscape architects are not in a position to provide that silence. The noise from a road penetrates to about a kilometre on either side. Silence has become one of the scarcest commodites in our densely populated regions. Many people are willing to pay for an expensive journey in order to experience it, and high prices are sometimes paid for remaining patches of undeveloped land, for the sake of preserving an area of silence in a reserve.

The same principle applies to our nose. We prefer to smell fresh air, without dust and without petrol fumes. The scent of dune vegetation, heathlands and pine forests refreshes us spiritually and physically. Fresh sea air is an article around which an entire recreation industry has grown up.

But the main thing about a landscape is that it includes everything we see: a far-off line of woodland or a hamlet in the distance. A winding road with trees or a farm embowered in greenery. The grazing cattle, the fields, earth banks overgrown with bushes and a solitary old tree. But it is also the bare straight lanes of asphalt and cement which neither man nor animal can cross with impunity any more, the higgledy-piggledy structures littered here and there, the refuse heaps, lamp standards, used-car dumps and all that shabby, dreary squalor which characterizes the areas that have been taken over by twentieth century man.

How much is it worth to us to be able to live in a landscape with many trees? Payne, a forestry economist, and Strom, a landscape architect in the USA discovered the answer by comparing the market value of an identical building plot with varying amounts of woodland. The difficulty was finding plots with a varying amount of vegetation and which were otherwise alike in every detail. In practice this proved to be almost impossible. They solved the problem by making a

small scale model of an existing building plot on the lines used
by builders of large edifices for obtaining a preview of a
project's actual appearance. This kind of scale model was
made of a piece of ground without vegetation about half a
hectare in area, which was earmarked for the building of
fourteen detached houses, near the town of Amhurst,
Massachusetts. It was photographed from various angles
after 0%, 33%, 66% and 100% of the terrain had been
studded with trees. These photographs were then sent to
sixteen different real-estate valuers together with a full
description of the building plot and the surroundings including, for example, the location of nearby schools, shops and
businesses and so on. Photographs of the real building plot
were also included.

The result was unmistakable. Whereas the real site without
vegetation was estimated at about £780 ($1,490) per acre on
the average (in 1975), the estimated value rose in proportion
with the amount of vegetation to a sum of £1,080 ($2,050), for
land two-thirds of whose surface area was wooded. When a
comparison was made between woodland in one block or
scattered over the whole site, the latter was preferred. A site
entirely covered in woodland was valued less highly than the
plot two-thirds covered: this was in connection with the
expense of removing the trees in preparing the ground for
development in the places were houses were to stand.

The experiment showed that, in this case, the presence of
woodland alone resulted in a 30% increase in site value for the
people living in this neighbourhood. This was, in addition to
the many other functions which nature fulfills, the economic
value of nature as a 'supplier of landscape beauty'.

In 1976 a large western European city spent nearly £35,700
on trees. Ir. A. Raad's method of estimating the value of
urban trees, on the basis of expenses incurred, is gaining
ground. For example, he worked out the value of the large
plane trees planted for the 1928 Olympic Games in
Amsterdam as follows:
Trunk diameter 415 cm. Site: city centre; condition: 100%;
spacing: ample. The formula is: unit price × species value ×

site value × condition value × planting method value = aesthetic value.

The *unit price* is a trade price amounting to £0.67 per cm² (in 1970) of the transverse section at a height of 1.30 metres. The *species value* depends on the rarity. Alders, poplars and willows are rated at 40%, all the rest at 100%. *Site value* relates to the environment, city trees being obviously more valuable than rural woodland trees. The *planting method value* is self-evident. The order for both these latter values is: *site:* – city centre 100%, urban area 90%, semi-urban area 80%, city limits 70%, rural area 60%. *Planting method*: solitary, 100%, street trees 80%, groups of 2–5 60%, large groups 40% and in wooded parks 20%. The *condition value* reflects the tree's health. Thus the formula for the Olympian plane trees is:

$$\text{diameter} = \frac{\text{circumference of trunk}}{\pi = 3.14} = \frac{4.15}{3.14} = 132 \text{ cm}$$

$$\text{radius} = \frac{\text{diameter}}{2} = \frac{132}{2} = 66 \text{ cm.}$$

$$\text{surface} = r^2 \times 3.14 = 66^2 \times 3.14 =$$
$$= 13.674 \text{ cm}^2$$

$$\text{surface} \times \quad £0.67 = \text{unit price} = \quad £9.156$$

The remaining values are all 100%, so the aesthetic value here equals the unit price. This only gives an estimated value based on investments, not on functions or use possibilities.

Various forest products

For centuries humankind has used nature to satisfy its need for food, fuel, medicines and domestic products. This is usually taken for granted. But the average urbanised westerner has become so alienated from nature, that many people have lost every direct association with it. A brief reminder of a random sample of the products we use seems appropriate.

ORCHIDS

The total number of orchid species is estimated at 15,000–20,000, about a thousand of which are found on Java. There is a network of dealers all over Indonesia, charging over £50 for some varieties. It is often difficult to grow orchids oneself, but the local people are often willing to go out and collect them in the forests

A trading company called 'Rands Orchids' recently issued large advertisements of a 'dramatic offer' of three new species of orchids from the jungles of Vietnam, India and the Philippines. Dramatic indeed, especially for the orchids. Collectors do not spare their favourites, so for plants and animals Charlotte Bronte's saying, 'I can be on guard against my enemies, but God deliver me from my friends!' is very apt. It is sometimes said that it is unlikely that orchids will be eradicated, because growers in temperate zones can produce sufficient seedlings to meet the demand. Yet many species have already disappeared. In 1932, a plan was sent to the Netherlands Commision for International Nature Conservation, suggesting that the Gulung Kelam in West Borneo should be declared an orchid reserve, because rare species grew there. Before this could be done, dealers got to hear of the proposal and organized a large expedition at short notice. The plants gathered were half decayed on arrival and only fetched about £11. After this, the reserve was no longer needed. There were no orchids left there.

The primeval forest could provide a supply of these valuable plants, but this capital is being destroyed too. In 1973, the orchids were given some protection from commerce by the 'Washington Convention on International Trade in Endangered Species of Wild Fauna and Flora'. Fifty-seven countries originally signed the convention. Over forty-eight have now ratified.

TREES

Trees belonging to the genus *Prosopis* present us with a good
example of species providing an abundance of products at
economic value. Their wood is used for fuel, gateposts and
paving blocks. Tannin is obtained from the bark and medicine from the inner bast. The pods provide cattle-fodder,
which is rich in protein, and the pod meal is used in baking
biscuits and bread and in making beer and molasses. A very
high quality honey is produced from the flowers and beeswax
is a common by-product because swarms of bees like to live
near them. The wood of some *Prosopis* species can be used for
the hardest and strongest household articles and even for
boats. And all this in Mexico, Peru, Argentine, Ecuador,
Ethiopia, the Sudan and other parts of the tropics.

The same applies to thousands of other species of trees,
Pithecollobium (with over 100 species) provides material for
cattle-fodder, lemonade, molasses, dyestuffs, gum, tannin.
Pterocarpus (over 100 species e.g. sandalwood) wood smells
of roses and is used in expensive furniture. *Robina* (locust
tree) provides a durable hard wood, formerly used for
mortice-and-tenon joints in wooden ships instead of nails.
The pins of the glass insulators on telegraph poles (these are
usually porcelain in England) are still made from this wood.
Sesbania has aromatic leaves used in foodstuffs and medicines. From *Sophora* (e.g. the Pagoda tree) we obtain dyes
and opiates for pharmacy, woods for wagons and tools, and,
of course, the flowers are used by honey-bees. The famous
Tamarind of Indonesia provides wood for charcoal and
furniture, pods and seeds for beverages, chutneys and medicines. Still in Indonesia, we find the nutmeg tree, which
produces both nuts and mace. An oil from the seeds of the
nutmeg is used in the perfume, tobacco and pharmaceutics
industries. There is a fat too, called nutmeg butter, which is a
constituent in candles and creams. These trees only grew wild
here until the sixteenth century. First the Portuguese and
then the Dutch collected them and made plantations. The
importance of the discovery is demonstrated by the history of
the trade with the East Indies, on which the prosperity of the

Dutch was founded for centuries! The spices, (including nutmeg and mace), were of the utmost importance.

Of the laurel trees, countless species, most of which are still nameless, grow in the American and Indian tropics, and possess many properties advantageous to man. Rosewood (rhodium), for example, provides oil for the perfume industry, medicines and flavouring for foodstuffs (such as bay leaves and cinnamon). Camphor, of great importance to pharmacy, is also derived from a species of laurel. The liquid amber (sweet gum) furnishes about the same products. For three thousand years or more, a resin called storax has been obtained from this tree. It is often used in the manufacture of perfumes, cosmetics, incense, lacquers, tobacco products and pharmaceuticals. From the witch-hazel, *Hamamelis*, an expensive astringent extract is obtained from the twigs and leaves. When incisions are made in an American maple a sweet liquid oozes out. This is the famous maple syrup, which is consumed on such a large scale, especially in the United States. Scandinavian fir trees produce an oil which has become an important raw material in vegetable margarine. *Acacias* provide the basic constituents for gum arabic, tannin, fibres, dyes, perfume oil (from the flowers), leather tanning substances, inks, wood for musical instruments, rope, mats and medicinal products. A particularly interesting tree is the *Albizia*, one species of which, *Albizia falcata*, can grow to a height of more than thirty metres, even on poor soil, within ten years. At that height, the crown resembles a giant parasol and provides indispensible shade in coffee and tea plantations where the *Albizia* grows between the crops.

Even more impressive is *Sequoia sempervirens*, the tallest tree in the world, of which the largest specimen ever found was 112 metres high and eight metres in diameter. Its age is estimated at about 2000 years. The wood of the *Sequoia*, also called the Redwood, is the finest to be found anywhere.

PALMS

The palm shows very clearly what a great effect a tree can have on a culture. In large parts of the world, palm trees have influenced the entire economic and cultural pattern of life of the population. They provide oil, wine, sugar, sago, meal, copra, fats and building materials, to mention but a few products. They retain water, provide shade in the driest and most arid regions of the earth, moderate the local climate and shelter the first growth of ground cover plants which are so essential for obtaining a layer of humus on dried-up or exhausted ground.

Eight hundred and one products of a large Indian fan palm are named in a poem; among them a medicinal alcoholic drink, food (seeds), roofing, fibres for mats, baskets and rope. Also of Indian origin is a wine palm which can produce up to twelve litres of sugary liquid every day in arid regions.

Two of the better known palms are the sago palm and the date palm. The first produces a starch which is the staple diet of many peoples of the world while, in the West it is chiefly used as a binding agent. A similar palm has such hard seeds that they are economically important as 'vegetable ivory', used for buttons.

For the inhabitants of the Arabian countries, Asia Minor and India, the date palm has been the most important converter of solar energy into nutritious oils for thousands of years. Many species and varieties of date palm exist, and it has been cultivated for centuries. Apart from food, this palm provides hundreds of other goods important to the lives of the local population. In recent years, large date palm plantations have been established in developing countries such as Persia and Iran, and also in America (New Mexico and Arizona). The species are improved by cross-breeding with wild species with an unnatural selection for the most desirable characteristics of the latter.

Raffia is naturally not a product to shake world economy. But some countries, including Malagasy and Mozambique, would be sorry to see the raffia palm disappear because it accounts for over 20% of their foreign currency. There is scarcely any question of cultivation though; the raffia palm is nature's tree.

In recent years, the economic significance of some natural

products has decreased, especially because of the rise of the chemical industry. Synthetic substitutes can now be manufactured from petroleum, coal, natural gas and other resources. This has given people a misconception of the meaning of 'synthetic'. Literally, it means 'put together'. It is popularly taken to mean 'artificial', suggesting 'technical, modern and disconnected from nature'. The effect is an alienation from nature. A widely-held view is 'We don't need natural products, we can manage very well with synthetics'.

But this view ignores the fact that synthetic products are merely combinations of natural products to which a certain chemical technique is applied. The natural products you start with are often fossils, but by no means always. Rayon, or artificial silk, has been made from wood fibre for the last eighty years. One day, this technical processing of natural products will come to an end, because the raw materials are no longer available. The enormous growth of the chemical industry, which has concentrated on the production of synthetics, could only take place because of the plentiful supplies of cheap wood, oil, coal and gas. This had important consequences:

–the production of the real natural articles became less for domestic use and more for export;
–the production dropped;
–the neglect of the wooded environment increased;
–the maintenance of forests became less important, and so they were cut down for 'never-to-be-repeated' profits;
–erosion increased;
–nature was destroyed.

Now that the price of oil has risen drastically (only to be followed by the prices of natural gas and of coal), the demand for some synthetics will decrease proportionally followed by a renewed demand for natural garments, for example, already perceptible in the cotton sector, and the search is on in remote areas of Central America for wild species with which to improve our existing breeds. Nature's importance in this respect cannot be overstated. There is no exaggeration in stating that civilization owes its existence to nature, and *still* cannot exist without it.

The responsibility should not lie with conservationists to show the government or anyone else that nature's functions are worth so much that they may not be destroyed. On the contrary, the burden of proof should lie with the *economists* to justify any destruction they encourage for the sake of production. The loss of yields and the damage caused to science, culture, the climate, food supplies and public health must all be accounted for. And we should be told why humankind, who has been drawing on nature's supplies for centuries, should have to stop doing so when, properly managed, the Earth could remain a supplier.

Eleven. Wildlife Stock Management

'Conservation is not a barrier to economic and social development, but rather an aid'.
President Pérez of Venezuela, 1974

Most nature lovers do not want to see nature as a utility article but as an isolated, untouchable system, available only to an elite body of experts. It is likely that this attitude has encouraged a greater alienation of nature from the urban masses than there would have been if the attitude was that nature belongs to everyone, especially to the local people. Those nature lovers who erect a psychological barrier of exclusiveness around the nature of tropical countries cause as much injury there as the poachers or woodcutters. They forget that, in the long run, nature conservation is only possible if it is accompanied by a general awareness that nature is worth conserving. Shutting people out of their local natural areas is asking for neglect, jealousy and vandalism.

In many countries, there is a growing conflict between the interests of nature on the one hand and the increases in prosperity and population on the other. The international conservation movement is coming to realize that a limited number of pockets of nature is all that may be left. However necessary the conservation endeavour may be, it does not stand a ghost of a chance in a situation of conflict which grows keener as population and hunger increase.

Conservation of nature must remain the principal object, but we must accept that it can only succeed if it is in accordance with the needs of the world population. If a community is hungry, when there is no alternative (and often when there is), it will annex any natural area available for arable farming and hunting wild animals. The only kind of nature conservation which stands a chance of success in these circumstances is the kind which does not deny people income and food. This must be considered when trying to save forests and esturaries from the clutches of industry and agriculture. Sometimes conservation has to make concessions to interests which are, apparently, incompatible. But with careful planning, the extremes can sometimes be compatible after all. The economic and technical capacities of nature are what the exploiters must consider.

But what is to be done about the animal species threatened with extinction? What is the connection with a capital-interest relationship? And what is the value, and thus the possible yield, of mountain gorillas, Grevy's zebra, oryx antelopes or pelicans? On the face of it this presents few problems. At present, a tiger skin is easily worth about £10,000. There are still about 3,000 wild tigers left, so if you shoot all of them you earn £30 million before you can say 'knife' – at least in theory. Elephants, too are well worth it. Ivory fetches, on average, about £18 per kilo. Shoot all the elephants in the world, sell their ivory, and you stand to earn up to £1,000 million. And there are other wild animals which provide trophies whose profits can line the pockets of a few individuals for a short time.

But this does not indicate the economic value of these animals because here the 'factory' is sold along with the 'product'. 'A management of fools' is how some economists term it. And, using this method of calculation, there are countless species which are worth little, if anything, either dead or alive, on a commercial basis. Some zoos may trade in nightjars, spiny mice or speckled starfish, but this isn't significant.

Luckily nature is too complex to permit this kind of division of species values. In its natural habitat, an elephant is not more valuable than any other species, merely by virtue of the (ivory) tusks. And although elephants can have a devasting effect on the environment because of their size, they are no more or less important than any other species in the web of ecological relationships.

It is of course possible to eliminate some species from an ecosystem without it collapsing. *But nobody knows what intervention can be fatal for the whole system.* We still know too little. And all too often our knowledge comes from people who have made mistakes: felled too many trees of an apparently important species, discharged too much warm industrial effluent, released too many harmful chemicals into the environment, exterminated predators, raised or lowered water levels, and all with familiar dismal consequences: animal species gone, plant cover gone, clean water gone, fertile soil gone, stability gone.

Generally speaking, a more stable and rich environment leads to a healthier agriculture and population. So that it is obviously beneficial to maintain the maximum stability expressed in *diversity* of animal and plant species, in any natural system. In seeking a dependent *permanent* direct relation between people and animals it is most important that people have a clear understanding that the stability of nature is in their own best interest.

Elephants

As with so many things, a strategy merely of preservation carried to extremes will defeat its own ends. In some East African reserves, for example, the vegetation is being destroyed because there are too many elephants and hippopotami. They are able to multiply unchecked, thanks to rigorous protection. Because the populations of predators such as lions and leopards have been so heavily depleted by man, the great herds of antelope upon which they prey are over-grazing the vegetation in some areas, so that both the animal and the habitat in which it lives suffer. Eventually this might lead to the collapse of the tourist industry in those countries where wildlife is the greatest attraction. And tourism is often a significant source of income. Kenya, for example, has an enormous tourist industry, worth considerably more than £50 million in 1972. More than any export item. The income from the stream of tourists can be regarded almost completely as the interest on the natural capital. On a five per cent basis, nature there already has a recreational value alone in the region of £1,000 million. But ignoring the fact that the animals attract observers from all over the world, they also provide a supply of meat, skins and ivory.

Kenya possesses about 120,000 elephants. Assuming that their average life-span is twenty-five years, and assuming an even distribution throughout the age range, this represents an annual mortality of 4,800 elephants. If we also assume an average yield in Kenya now of ten kilos per animal, this amounts to 48,000 kilos. Ivory fetches a high price. On the world market, and especially in the East, it has been playing the same role as gold and silver. At present, the average value of raw ivory (there are many grades) is about £18 per kilo, and perhaps £50 per kilo after processing (and very much more if a lot of work has gone into it); whereas silver and gold fetch about £85 and £2750 per kilo respectively. Ivory is not only a raw material for chess sets, statuettes and piano keys, but is also an investment object. This annual amount of 48,000 kilos of ivory ought to bring in more than £860,000 (two million dollars). On a five per cent interest basis, this indicates that the elephants present have an ivory-capital value of £17.2 million (40 million dollars.)

In practice, ivory is so valuable that it is impossible to prevent more animals being shot than is responsible for good management. For example, in the past the official export figures of Kenya have been far lower than the total listed by the ivory-importing countries. It seems probable from the figures that about 20,000 elephants were being killed every year. Fortunately, in 1977 Kenya outlawed the hunting of wild life. The effectiveness remains to be seen, but had this not happened a simple sum would show that both the tourist industry based on elephants and the export of ivory would have ceased to be a paying proposition within ten years.

Hoofed animals

The economic value of the African antelope herds, in tourism, is famous and is a good reason for ensuring their responsible management. But one value of the antelope has come to light comparatively recently and, in being important to the locals, gives fresh hope to the continued existence of some endangered species. We allude to a form of control called 'wildlife utilization' or 'wildlife stock management'. Harvesting some of the surplus of births over natural deaths of wild herds is far more efficient than pasturing domestic cattle in natural subtropical regions. This is all the more important since these wild species are under pressure from direct competition for land required for cattle-breeding and agriculture.

But the conditions required for the practice of agriculture rarely fit the special needs demanded by the local soil, flora and fauna. Many of the measures taken to improve conditions for cattle or arable farming lead to the erosion or destruction of the natural environment so that, in the long run, this form of 'development' means it will no longer be possible to use the ground at all: there will be no nature and no agriculture.

Stock raising has been carried out in these countries for centuries. In some communities the cattle are a status symbol above any other function. The more cattle a man has, the more important he is. But now that the number of people has increased, as well as their livestock, this custom has had (and still has) disastrous consequences. As domestic animals, the cattle are poorly adapted to the environment. They can properly use and digest only about 10% of the plant growth present, so that the useful yield of the growth available is low. What they do efficiently, however, is to ruin the soil through trampling, so that young shoots have no chance to grow up. The result of these two things is exhaustion and erosion. In poor countries, improvement of the conditions for breeding cattle is too expensive and complex.

A brilliant alternative is to use native species of hoofed animals. Having evolved in the natural environment over thousands of years, they are beautifully adapted to their habitat and very efficient in obtaining a high yield from the available plant growth. Both UNESCO and IUCN have assessed some of the advantages of this kind of stock management and, above all, have investigated its feasibility in relation to the maintenance of the natural environment in those countries. It has been found that nature conservation and economic profit can co-exist better than was ever thought possible.

Considering how arid the regions are, it is remarkable that the biomass per square kilometre is as high as 15,000 kilos for Kenya, 18,000 to 31,000 kilos for Uganda and 2,000 to 6,000 kilos for other East African countries. In North America the figure was 2,400 to 3,500 kilos per square kilometre before the bison were almost exterminated. The only animals which can improve the yield in these countries (albeit temporarily) are goats, which reach 50,000 kilos per square kilometre. Friesian cattle also reach a higher figure. But it is a lame comparison, because goats do not leave a blade of vegetation and are literally flora-predators. And the breeding of cattle requires intensive irrigation and other care, so that the relationship with the natural environment is completely lost. Wild hoofed animals (ungulates) are superior 'gardeners' by comparison. They eat in a way which enables the plant to flower afresh. Overcropping of flora occurs only in the unnatural circumstances of there being too many grazers. Every species has its own preference so that, instead of 10%, as with ordinary cattle rearing, 80–90% of the vegetation is utilised. As a rule, domestic cattle convert much food into fat, but in tropical countries a great deal is needed to produce the kinetic energy used to cover great distances in search of drinking water.

Game animals are not wasteful and produce more useful protein than cattle. Scanty water supplies are a daily problem for cattle. However, the water requirement of game is adapted to the likelihood of finding water or to the supply in their own territory. Some species of antelope do not require any drinking water. Feeding habits, behaviour and physical characteristics are adapted to an optimal use of dew, vege-

tation rich in moisture, cooler hours of the day and fluctuations of temperature. They do not sweat, produce very dry
dung, and only obtain water from the plants they eat. So these
species, such as oryx and addax, can thrive under very arid
conditions which domestic cattle could not hope to survive.
Wild ungulates have the additional advantage that they
mature much more rapidly than cattle, and so produce more
yield from their natural capital at a faster rate, because sexual
maturity is reached earlier.

Finally, with wild animals, natural selection provides for a
maximal resistance to diseases and other hazards of life in
nature. But in tropical and subtropical countries especially,
because of the unsuitable living conditions, cattle suffer from
all kinds of diseases.

Wildlife stock management is already being practised here
and there on a small scale. The best example is the Russian
saiga antelope. At one time, millions of these animals used to
live on the steppes of Russia, but they were almost eliminated
by wholesale poaching until, by 1922, only 1,000 were left.
Since that time the saiga has been under the protection of a
careful management policy. By 1976 the total wild population
had increased to over two million. The annual interest of this
enormous natural capital consists of six million kilos of good
quality meat, enormous quantities of first class leather and
suede, oil and raw materials for pharmaceutics, cosmetics and
other products. The by-product of the saiga is the maintenance of the Russian and Siberian steppes.

The reindeer culture of the Lapps and the caribou of the
Eskimos are also examples of large-scale stock management,
whereby a certain relationship exists between economic profit
and the preservation of an animal species in its natural
environment. Yet the possibilities for wildlife management
in Africa are far greater, its most attractive feature being the
fact that endangered habitats and species can be saved at the
same time, and that the protein production will be an obvious
benefit to the hungry locals.

Vicuna

One more example, this time from Latin America. Not only meat but also wool can be harvested from wild animals. The vicuna is a small, slender cousin of the Llama, and inhabits the mountains of Peru, Bolivia, Chile and Argentina. Not long ago, they became very rare indeed, because of the value of their fleece, the finest and softest that is known. In the summer they graze in the high, bare mountains where ordinary cattle-breeding is out of the question, but in other seasons they compete for grazing land, although their food requirements are not the same as those of cattle and sheep. They nibble at their food, and can crop small plants which other animals cannot get at.

The vicuna graze in small groups, one male with a number of females. The male stands on look-out, and when danger threatens, he gives the signal for rapid flight and leads the herd. The hunters know this and start by shooting the male so that the females run about undecidedly and can easily be picked off one by one. Because the vicuna is now protected in reserves and, in commerce, by the international convention on trade in endangered species, the numbers have increased to about 60,000. In the large reserve called Pampa Galeras, in Peru, the number of animals, which had fallen to 600 in 1961, has arisen to 20,000, thanks to protection and good management. Yet this has not solved the problem. In the long term, it will not be possible to protect the animals simply by these means alone. The commercial value of the animal is so high that, as with the elephant and rhinoceros, poachers will go to extraordinary lengths to obtain their quarry. Yet it is not necessary to kill for the wool. The old Incas took the yield without destroying their capital. When it was time to harvest the wool, the people used to take drums and form themselves into an enormous circle. Sometimes as many as thirty thousand people took part in this ritual. The animals were slowly herded together and caught by hand. After they had been shorn they were set free again.

Felipe Benavides, a nature conservationist, wants to revive

this system on modern lines. The Incas did it on foot because they had no horses. (These were imported from Europe later). Nowadays the vicuna can be driven together by horsemen and funnelled by fences of nylon gauze into a small enclosed space. With this system the animals are not killed and the wool is processed centrally in one factory. The people obtain their share of the profit on the basis of land ownership, and this amounts to more than they would be able to obtain from hunting.

The objection to this kind of approach to nature conservation is well-known: nature and the noble animal itself would be degraded to a piece of vulgar commercial merchandize! Reality teaches us that ethical or even techno-biological arguments are seldom enough to prevent the plundering of nature. One must accept that the side-effect of a practical economic approach is that nature not only continues to exist but is kept in a healthy state. What more can you want?

Twelve. On the Boundary Between Land and Sea

Between us and hell or heaven there is nothing but life which of all things is the frailest.

Blaise Pascal

The function of estuaries

Our little island of Terschelling lies on the northern boundary of an immense area, which is neither sea nor land: the Wadden. It is one of the richest areas of tidal regions and estuaries in the world, extending for tens of thousands of square miles, from Holland along the Friesian, West German and part of the Danish coast. Twice in every twenty-four hours, a flood of life-bringing water surges through the tidal inlets between the many islands. The water is rich in silt, oxygen and food to sustain hundreds of organisms, including many species of birds. Together with the East Scheldt in Zeeland and the Wash and Thames estuary of England's east coast, the Wadden contains the most important coastal waters of the North Sea and the largest estuary in the world.

It is threatened by reclamation, dyke-building, oil and gas borings, river pollution, industrial effluent pipes, army manoeuvres, harbour extensions, industrial sites and power stations penetrating the estuaries. In 1974 the Dutch Economic Institute, in assessing the economic advantages of reclamation for harbour construction in the Balgzand, (a small area of the Wad near Den Helder), the economic value of this area in its natural state was put at no more than £890 per hectare, which is also the price paid for marginal agricultural land. So the reclamation would not mean a serious loss of capital. £890 is nothing compared with the value of the same area when harbours and factories have been built. Thanks to this kind of assessment, the Wadden region has become fair game for developers, and industry has been given a free hand. But the calculation is quite irrelevant, which is not surprising considering the rarity of economists who consider nature in their calculations.

The annual yield of the estuaries can be calculated at £4,445 per hectare (1975), at least – a value many times higher than the out-dated assessment made by the Dutch Economic Institute.

Our figures come from three reports about estuaries: *The value of the tidal marsh* by an American ecologist, E. P. Odum; and two Dutch reports, one on the East Scheldt and the other on the Wadden Sea. Their common point of departure lies in the need to describe the economic and ecological values of estuaries in their natural state and, if possible, to weigh them against the alternatives of harbour construction and industrialization. With this in mind, the estuaries were analyzed for their biological, chemical, recreational and productive values, which were expressed in monetary terms as far as possible.

More often than not, the true value of natural waters is not accounted for when possible uses have to be weighed against one another. The most common choices for administrators are between such alternatives as harbour construction, reclamation for agricultural land, a new airport or a recreational project. The natural state of the water plays no part in the debate, because familiar and calculable figures do count and the emotions of people who find small birds and fishes more important than the growth of production do not.

In addition, the great usefulness of our estuaries is not always experienced on the spot but out at sea, via fisheries and economic activities dependent on them. And so it is easy to forget that these activities would be impossible if the estuary were turned into an industrial site.

It is estimated that over 45% of the net primary production of small organisms, for any given estuary, disappears into the sea with the ebbing tide. Some of these organisms are snapped up there by the secondary producers, the fish. As well as the ebb and flow from the oceans, most estuaries also have connections with rivers flowing into them or marshes in the coastal area and other shallow waters upstream. These export organic and mineral nutrients to the estuary, where they are deposited and consumed. Thus the production of organisms in the estuary is dependent on distant water areas, and the visible yields often become apparent far away from the estuary itself. This inter-connection is sometimes hard to understand, because many people simply do not find it easy to visualize the complicated, perpetually-moving mechanisms. of nature, both in space and time. What is near and familiar can be taken in at a glance, but what is far away presents no immediate problem and so is disregarded. On top of this, the estuary's yields do not benefit the owners, whether they are private individuals or governments, but benefit the people in other countries or the (sometimes foreign) fishermen far out at sea. This is a horrible complication for a cost and revenue analysis, because a capital has to be administered by people who do not receive its interest. Thus the natural estuary-capital acquires an international significance which is not apparent when making a normal computation of the possible yield of alternative uses of the estuary. These seemingly incomparable quantities must be compared: the yield from an industry to be set up in one's own interests in the short term, versus the yield from the natural biological system on behalf of others in short and long terms. Usually, the first interest prevails, and so coastal marshes disappear.

As a result the Netherlands has already lost large parts of the Wadden, California has lost 67% of its coastal marshes, and the states of New York and New Jersey have lost 10–25%. In England, nearly 30% of the most important estuaries and coastal marshes fell into the hands of industrial developers between 1965 and 1973.

The reports referred to above list very many functions of estuaries – the following are the main four:

1 Use as nurseries for the fishery, and breeding-places for

shellfish cultivation;

2 Recreational significance for sport fishermen, water sportsmen, bird-lovers, those who simply seek peace and quiet;

3 Purification of waste water; and

4 They play a key role in the bio-chemical cycles of life on earth. Odum calls this the 'life support function'.

These functions are described more fully in the following section, with the exception of recreation, which is dealt with in another chapter.

FISHERY

Two thirds of the world's catch of fish consists of species of fish whose hatchlings grow to maturity in tidal areas. Without these nurseries the young fishes would not thrive, and the fishery would shrink to a fraction of its present size. In 1968, the world fish catch amounted to 64,000 million kilos. Only a part of the value of this lays in the earnings of the fishermen, which average about eleven pence a kilo. The sorting, auctioning, transportation, in some cases processing, and all the other things that happen to fish, all go to increase the price per kilo ten-fold by the time it retails in the shops. And the economic utility of the fishery is not yet exhausted. There is the building of fishing vessels and equipment to take into account, as well as the industries which supply the food industry with processing and transport. But for the sake of this calculation, we will restrict ourselves to the market price of a little over £1 per kilo. The total turnover amounts to over £70,000 million. More than £43,000 million of this originates in the estuaries sheltering the hatchlings. In spite of this, the fishery value of the estuaries is often dismissed as unimportant. It is associated with seamen who live in isolated villages, reek of fish, and work when townsmen are still lying in bed. The fishery is still always associated with cold and dirt, and not with the much-desired image of big business. But a single figure may help the image. If the world's catch of fish, shrimps and shellfish, amounting to £65,000 million (probably an underestimate) is regarded as an interest of 5%

on the natural fish capital, then that capital might be put at £131,000 million.

The size of this capital and the extent to which people depend on it, can be seen in the dramatic history of the Peruvian anchoveta fishery, which was the largest in the world until 1972, thanks mainly to the rich coastal fishing grounds. In 1971, Peru still had a fish yield of 10.6 million tons, but in 1972 it dropped suddenly to 4.8 million tons. The reasons for this rapid decline are not entirely clear. One theory is that there was a change in the natural conditions, such as a change of temperature, causing the plankton, which the anchovies eat, to disappear. But the most popular view considers the enormous population fluctuations of the anchovies as the key. Over-fishing has certainly occurred, and a mixture of natural population crash with continuous over-fishing is disastrous for the stocks. Recovery can depend on the success of reproduction from a single year. If this does not come off – and with continued heavy fishing it is unlikely to – then the stocks collapse altogether after a series of bad years. The fishery becomes unprofitable and so has to stop. This is just as well for the fish stocks, which may need many years to build up again to a normal level – if they can at all.

Whales can be exterminated because they reproduce slowly and because, wherever they seek refuge, they eventually have to surface for air. Common species of fish can become scarce through over-fishing; sole and herring, for example, which have almost disappeared from the North and Irish Seas, but provided that they remain above their critical survival level, below which there is no chance of recovery, and there is only a moderate fishery, their stocks may again reach a reasonable level eventually. One way to ensure the irreparable decline of these species is to destroy their nurseries, by polluting the estuaries and coastal waters for instance, or reclaiming them for land.

The legendary fishes of the European rivers disappeared many years ago because their spawning grounds were destroyed. As late as 1885, 104,000 salmon were brought to the fish auction near Rotterdam. A gigantic quantity, which brought wealth to the fishermen while the public benefitted. After barrages were built in the river Maas, the salmon could no longer reach their spawning grounds upstream. It was a fate which the salmon shared with such fish as sturgeon and shad, millions of which were present throughout the rivers of Western Europe in the last century. They did not disappear because of pollution however, which only came much later, but because the spawning grounds were destroyed.

The current answer to these pleas to preserve the estuaries is that technology is quite capable of finding a replacement for the nursery function, and that fish can be cultivated in increasing numbers. Thus the 'free' service of nature has to make way for technological systems, which might bring about a great increase in fish production. According to the UN *Development Forum*, the world production of fish in the coming twenty years could be increased to a 150 million tons in this way; more than double the present quantity. This kind of announcement is what economists love, because they understand it, a technically-controlled and limited fish hatchery system of which simple input-output analyses can be made, whose yields can be sold and the profits counted. But there is a flaw in the argument. A technological system of this sort is expensive and difficult to run, because it is impossible to imitate exactly the ecology of the estuaries; certainly it cannot be done on the enormous scale which has been envisaged. There are also problems with the domestication of species unsuitable for cultivation, problems which no technology can solve. And so it is the more surprising that economists prefer the expensive man-made contrivance to the free and efficient services of nature.

The economic importance of shellfish harvesting is not rated very highly as a rule, although every country with any sizeable estuaries has thousands of people earning a living from it. According to Odum, estuaries such as the East Scheldt, the Wadden, the Wash and the Thames estuary have a net annual turnover of £1,700 per hectare from shellfish (1974), over and above the capital value calculated from the nursery function.

PURIFICATION OF WASTE WATER AND EFFLUENT

Because water is, fortunately, gradually coming to be looked on as precious, its purity is seen as the greatest treasure, and not to be tampered with. But, drinking water apart, a certain amount of waste-water is in fact, not only tolerable but also desirable, so long as there are no toxic substances which cannot be broken down, of course. The natural productivity of the water is increased by organic waste matter, which heightens the economic value of the biological system. Some degree of organic pollution, for example, is actually favourable for the shrimp fishery off the North Sea coasts. It does not necessarily follow that dirty waste-water in the Wadden Sea and East Scheldt leads to a polluted coast or a contaminated estuary. Nutrients brought down by the rivers always have collected in these waters and their biological purifying capacity is surprisingly great. Therefore the fairly common idea that this purification service is incompatible with the fishery function (including the catch of oysters and mussels) is ill-founded. For the functions would only be competing if too much toxic waste-water were discharged. This might increase the primary production to a certain extent (it is a question of nutrients), but it would thus cause overloading finally, resulting in deoxygenation and 'dead' water.

Clearly, then, there is a limit to the waste-water treatment function. Below this limit, the ecosystem remains intact, the water remains reasonably pure, the estuary retains its nursery function and the waste-water can be discharged. However, it is important that more than 98% of the material in the waste-water should always be organic, thus able to be broken down biologically (bio-degradable). This is *not* the case with the Rhine.

We can make a financial estimate of an estuary's purification function by comparing it with the costs of building and maintaining water purification plants, which actually do no more than imitate nature, in a poor way. In making the calculation it becomes obvious that the estuaries we mention do the work of several thousand purification plants, with the additional advantages that there are no building or running costs, they do not use fossil energy but direct solar energy, and they have many other pleasant uses. The American report, calculating the value of the waste-water treatment function of an estuary in this way, estimates it at £15,000 per hectare per annum. Together with yields of other functions, this brings the value of such a small area of sea to several thousands of millions of pounds if, as usual, we capitalize the yields against an interest rate of 5% per annum.

This free service is underrated simply because the outsider has no idea how great the achievement of nature is. The technical evolution described earlier has encouraged an ever-increasing alienation from nature. The vast importance of nature's services is no longer seen; it is taken for granted as endless and over-estimation, over-fishing and pollution are the results.

The purification capacity of water can be measured by the 'Biological Oxygen Demand' (BOD). This figure gives the quantity of oxygen used by a system in processing a certain amount of pollution. What makes the estuary so exceptional is the 'third step' purification in which nature extracts the nutrient salts, especially phosphates, from the water, and fixes them in living matter. It would cost over £13,000 a year to perform this by artificial means.

However, one should not use these extreme figures as a yardstick because, in practice, the result of a maximal use of the purifying capacity would entail an inadmissible decrease of the other functions such as fisheries and recreation. Therefore a balance has to be found. The phosphates, which are the most important nutrient salts, are effectively dispersed by the tides and used in the biological cycle. Silt and sand serve as a storeroom for stocks of surplus nutrient salts and even as a means of disposing of them altogether.

The buffer capacity is enormous, which is one of the main reasons why a very polluted river, such as the Belgian Scheldt, does not pollute the sea off the coast of Zeeland very much. It first passes through an estuary which is eighty kilometres long. Also there is an interchange of water between the Scheldt and the estuary of the East Scheldt, which is very stable biologically and has a cleansing function extending far beyond its own region.

The third-step purification in the man-made plants only deals with the phosphates. Nitrogen compounds, however, are an equally great source of pollution, and purification plants are unable to cope with these adequately. But in the deeper layers of estuarine mud, which are often devoid of oxygen, these *are* broken down with tremendous efficiency. Experiments show that, of 225 kilos of phosphates and 280 kilos of nitrogen deposited per acre (about 0.4 hectares), 200 kilos of phosphates and 250 kilos of nitrogen has disappeared within a few months. Because modern society cannot cope without phosphates and nitrogen, but it is expensive or even impossible to remove them by technical means, estuaries should be valued far more highly than they are. They perform this service while all their other functions continue. The total value is hundreds of thousands of pounds per hectare.

The loss of the Dutch Biesbosch, for instance, as the only freshwater tidal area in Western Europe, has never previously been looked at in this light, although it was an estuary which made a great contribution to the purification of the water in the Rhine and Maas delta. For the same reasons, the loss of the Zuyder Zee, and many other shallow coastal seas all over the world have had economic results which have never appeared on any balance sheet.

THE 'LIFE-SUPPORT' FUNCTION

The biochemical processes of estuaries are technically inimitable but are as indispensible as oxygen for breathing and water for drinking. Odum calls their activity the 'life-support' function.

The biosphere is not a static thing, but a gigantic active laboratory in which no pipe may be wrongly connected and no retort stand in the wrong place. Here the chemical processes take place which make life possible or, if disturbed, destroy that life. The plants which grow thanks to photosynthesis also need nitrogen as well as carbon dioxide and water. Nitrogen is extracted from the air by bacteria and assimilated into the living organisms. Plants such as clover, lupins and beans are very important in this respect, because nitrogen-fixing bacteria live in the nodules on their roots.

After a lengthy passage through the plant and animal kingdoms, including humans, these nitrogen compounds are again reduced to simpler forms, such as ammonia, and finally back to nitrogen again. The carbon conversion takes place with the aid of sun and water, but for the nitrogen cycle, micro-organisms (bacteria) are necessary at the beginning and end of the process. If they cannot do their work properly, then disturbances occur. A disturbance can lead to a nitrogen surplus upsetting the system so that toxic substances accumulate. Or it could lead to a shortage, which hinders the early development of the food chains, and the ultimate result is protein deficiency and hunger. To a limited extent, artificial fertilizers can be used to improve nitrogen fixation, but a very large amount of nitrogen is needed, whereas the extent of the natural nitrogen fixation cannot, so far as is known, be approached by human technological expertise.

Investigations have shown that the estuaries are ideal areas for these processes, so great is their efficiency. The largest chemical factories on earth are nature's.

Then there is also the sulphur cycle, and again the estuaries provide an important link. Industry contributes about a third of the total sulphur content in the atmosphere. Sometimes rain combines with the sulphur dioxide in the air and turns into sulphuric acid, but it is surprisingly infrequent. Most of the sulphur it seems is deposited and retained. It occurs in the deeper deoxygenated layers of mud and silt in the estuary, where the noxious sulphur is converted into other harmless sulphur compounds. If this did not happen, the sulphuric acid would, as it were, 'burn' the surroundings. Plants, animals and objects – and our lungs too of course – are not prepared for the reception of sulphuric acid. Nearly all the surplus sulphur on land is eventually washed down to the sea, and causes damage on the way. Nature converts the sulphur into more innocuous compounds in silt and in the estuaries.

What then is the value of this 'laboratory'? Estimation is made more difficult because the process goes on all round the world. But, like every single natural function, from which profit can be derived indefinitely, the life-support function should be assigned an infinite value. However, one can make a kind of spot check. It ought to be a matter of course that, when plans are being made to set up industry in estuaries, the cost to the community of replacing the laboratory and other functions at that time should be worked out. It is usually possible to draw up a balance of the useful functions (and thus of the benefits) of the estuary, and of the eventual losses. The part played by the presence of a shallow coastal sea in reducing the damage caused by sulphuric acid can also be calculated.

A comparison of the natural production of nitrogen with the production by human agents shows that in one hectare of estuary, rich in silt, nature's achievement is approximately as great as that of three medium-sized fertilizer factories. The costs and yields of these factories indicate the value of the estuary's chemical functions. It is only a rough estimate though, for an important part of the nitrogen cycle cannot be replaced by artificial fertilizer. One of the most ironic possibilities, therefore, would be the sacrifice of an estuary for establishing an artificial fertilizer factory.

PROTECTION

A final function must be added to the estuary's list – that of protection against storm floods, because their wide, shallow water surface is a reservoir for high tides.

The energy of a stormy sea is often intercepted in estuaries and neutralized by the great sandbanks and the system of channels. This value is sometimes underestimated, because it is ignored that the money countries spend on protection against potential flood disasters is related to the flood-stemming function of the estuary. It is not always possible to demonstrate this relationship directly, because provisions have to be made at all times for coastal protection. But if an important estuary is closed off from the sea, all manner of side-effects take place along the coast, such as erosion, damage to dykes, scouring and subsidence. Reconstruction costs will then reflect the value of the estuary's 'water-buffer' function.

Beaches and harbours also benefit from the presence of estuaries. For the clean sand that is continually being thrown up to the beach generally proves to have been brought down from nearby estuaries. And when dams are constructed to close off shallow coastal waters from the sea, dredging operations usually have to be carried out non-stop just to keep adjacent harbours deep and accessible.

ENERGY

One of the most sensational new methods of calculating the economic value of nature has been worked out by H. T. and E. P. Odum. We do not yet know how useful this method will ultimately prove to be. Heated debates are still going on about it. Some people think it quite impracticable, while others consider it to be the obvious solution.

The 'Odum & Odum' method is based on the principle that energy flow from the sun runs through every natural system and is fixed in biomass (where biomass means the total mass of living things). This process is sometimes called the 'primary production'. This production is a good measuring rod for the efficiency of solar energy, because all life has a useful function, whether it be in grassland, wayside vegetation, woodlands, scrub, a tidal area or sea. But one only realizes the importance of primary production if one imagines how things would be if it did not exist. Its usefulness cannot be determined by any ordinary economic calculation. The answer depends on how much people are willing to pay for the product. Yet one cannot deny that it is essential, though it is far easier to work out the value of cucumbers produced in this way than that of algae in the sea or plants in an alpine meadow.

However, one can measure the primary production by calculating the amount of solar energy converted. Solar energy is free, but the carriers in which it is fixed – such as firewood, coal, oil and natural gas – are not (at least not to the consumer). In fact there is a close connection between the Gross National Product and the Gross Consumption of Energy, which makes it possible to establish a certain cost for a certain amount of energy. Thus in the United States, it appears that one dollar is equivalent to 10,000 kilojoules. So the energy flow of the primary production, generally expressed in joules, can also be reflected in monetary terms.

This seems more complicated than it is. *Old*, stored solar energy, in the form of fossil fuels and the resultant production, is entered in economic book-keeping without a second thought. But the energy flow coming from the sun *now* is equally important. The only difference is that the latter is free and for that reason economists will disagree about the *utility* of its production. One economic rule says that the 'economic subjects' have to express their 'preferences' for a product. If they do not there is no demand, no value is attributed to it and, thus, there is no supply. Following this idea to its natural conclusion, the sun is wasting its energy on something that has no utility and no value. This is a line of reasoning which nicely reflects both the essence and the limitations of economic theory.

So very little can be said against the Odum & Odum method. On the contrary, it fills the gap which cannot be seen by economists and which lies outside the ecologists field of view. The latter object that the practical application of this method results in a division into 'valuable' and 'valueless' landscapes. Poor areas, such as deserts, tundra, dunes and woodlands on sandy soil would come off very badly, because their primary production is relatively low.

This is true. However, conservationists who really want a measuring rod, with which to value and defend their paradises, will have to accept a certain order of precedence. For a virgin forest has a far greater diversity and stability than a savannah; an old estate is more important biologically than a dull plantation of fir trees. The Odum & Odum theory is not the only definition of value, and there are no objections to also pointing out the unique landscape value of a sand-drift, for example, or the recreational value of a dune area. There are other reasons than diversity or a high primary production for preserving these sort of areas.

Using the Odum & Odum method though, the value of an estuary comes out very high because the solar energy converted has a high return, with a large primary production. Expressed in the production-energy relation of the GNP, production in the estuary is worth approximately £28,500 per hectare a year.

There are many reasons why these production properties of nature are never termed 'economic' and some of them have already been mentioned. An additional reason is that most economists do not consider *all* the needs of a community, but restrict their view to the ordinary, everyday things like housing, motoring, road-building, shopping, holidays by air, industry and trade. The existence of natural production is not taken into account. But a national book-keeping, which only adds up how well-off we are (the National Income), is a mockery if the production of simple, consumer goods is at the expense of the biological conditions on which our existence rests.

Thirteen. Nature as the Inspiration of Culture

'One impulse from a vernal wood
May teach us more of man,
Of moral evil and of good,
Than all the sages can.'
                                    Wordsworth

Communication

Without nature, science and culture would be poorly developed. It is a source of inspiration for scientific investigation, art and recreation. This is extremely obvious but,
oddly enough, is seldom taken into account. Nature is
experienced more and more in an artificial form; so one can
easily imagine the flat-dweller on the tenth or twentieth floor
of his concrete colossus, which stands on the spot where a
wood used to grow, watching a television film about woods.

It seems, however, that nature can be offered as a rare
consumer article. This fact sometimes causes bitterness, but
it does encourage a business-like approach, for a consumer
article like this is naturally interesting economically. For
instance, the amount of broadcasting time which radio and
television devote to nature is enormous. To give a single
example: in February 1976, more than fifteen and a half hours
of radio air-time in the Netherlands were devoted to nature,
including programmes with a high audience rating and high
appreciation figures. This is about 3.5% of the total monthly
sound broadcasting time. In the same month, television put
out fourteen and a half hours of nature programmes – about
15% of the total monthly viewing time. The indirect attention to nature in other programmes ought to be added to this,
but it was not possible to itemize it.

Nature films are the basis of enormous undertakings, with thousands of millions of pounds involved, and companies such as Disney, Cousteau and Anglia. That some of these film-makers distort nature – Disney especially is a past master at this – does not detract from the fact that without it, these undertakings would not have any grounds for existence.

The great cultural trend of Romanticism, in which romantic man tried to identify himself and his roots, existed by the grace of nature. Both the literature and painting of the Romantic era were centred on nature, and even its music, such as Beethoven's Pastoral Symphony, was inspired by it. In 1775, when Romanticism was at its height, there was even a 'Temple of Nature' founded in the mountains near Chamonix, by nature-lovers whose love of nature had almost become a religion.

In 1976, tens of thousands of pounds were paid for picturesque landscape panels dating from the Romantic period. Economists will of course suggest that the price does not necessarily include any appreciation for the *nature* represented but only concerns the rarity of the painting. This is almost certainly true, but without nature the picture could not have been painted, and without the romantic yearning for Arcadian nature which is reproduced, the work would not have been made at that time.

To what extent does nature supply subjects for literature? A new back-to-nature trend is evident in modern writings. We tried to verify this using a random sample from the Dutch Newspaper for the Book Trade, which lists all the works which appear in the bookshops. We counted the books published during December 1975 and June 1976, and ascertained how many of these would not have been written if nature had not existed. Of the 1221 titles, 175 had some bearing on nature. That is, over 14%. According to research carried out in this field, more than 40 million books were sold in the Netherlands in 1975, for which more than £128.8 million were paid. The average price per book was a little over £3. Calculated like this, the Dutch public would have spent more than £17.7 million on books about or connected with nature. But because the number of nature books printed and the price are often higher than average (as there are usually many plates and books of photographs), we can easily assume that the total sum will be far in excess of £22 million. We also have to consider that the trade newspaper does not list all publications that have appeared in the Netherlands, and text-books and scientific publications are not mentioned at all. A complete statement for each month is unobtainable, although this is not usually the case in other countries.

In West Germany, for example, according to the *Deutsche Nationalbibliographie*, 1651 books were published in December 1975, sixty-five of which (4%) dealt with nature. The average price price was 22.55 Dm.

For the same month, the *Bibliographie de France* named 542 publications, thirty-three of which (6%) were concerned with nature. The average price was sixty-four francs.

The American *Weekly Record* named 2836 new publi-cations, 4% of which were concerned with nature. The average price was $10.74.

On the basis of this admittedly superficial investigation, it appears that about one twentieth of the world output of books and other bound publications could not have been written without the existence of nature, and that about one seventh of what the man in the street reads is on this subject. The figures are astronomical!

It is commonly heard that this kind of cultural exploitation has a good chance of surviving even when the plants and creatures it exploits have died out. But this is questionable. In reality, both the devastated area and the extinct animal probably disappear from the cultural scene fairly quickly. Of course, there is always a time lag, when the item in question is referred to as if it was still there. After the Zuyder Zee in the Netherlands was closed off in 1932, this enormous freshwater estuary with its seals and wealth of herrings and anchovies remained in the thoughts and lives of the people for some years. But who remembers now how rich the Zuyder Zee, (now replaced by the smaller Ysselmeer), used to be? Who can still remember the buckling herring which lived there:

this species is now extinct, but was particularly good when smoked, so that it was once a speciality of the district.

Not so very long ago, different breeds of horses, poultry and cattle were found in every rural area. But these were ousted by uniformly-bred, highly productive breeds. The handsome, colourful fowl are only known now from old paintings, and do not exist in the cultural pattern of modern society.

In 1800, the passenger pigeon was still the most numerous species of bird in North America. In the old Indian cultures, it appears to have been a symbol of natural abundance. Towards the time of migration, the birds would flock together in such incredible numbers that the trees in which they roosted often collapsed under the weight. Indian tales tell how the sky was darkened by swarms of them migrating to the Caribbean coasts of Florida and Mexico. In 1810, the number of birds in a single flock was estimated at two million. And in the 1860s the total population is thought to have been 9,000 million. But between March and August 1878, 1.5 million passenger pigeons from one breeding colony were sent to New York to be eaten. Using traps and lime-twigs, nets, guns and even grenades, the people wreaked havoc among the pigeons. In addition, they had their natural enemies, whose numbers had fallen much less sharply.

On September 1, 1914, the last passenger pigeon, held in captivity, died in Cincinnati zoo. She was called Martha. It was just as if people only realized then what had happened. The little corpse was carefully frozen, and everything that could be done by way of measuring, photographing or sketching was done.

At first, the passenger pigeon remained a popular subject for publications and other cultural manifestations. The empty pigeon-house in the zoo was like a place of pilgrimage for quite a time. Voluminous text-books appeared about the remarkable Martha and the rather unexpected demise of her kind. But then it stopped. Apart from one or two precious, guarded, stuffed birds, the passenger pigeon has departed from the cultural scene for good.

Yet another example is the gigantic Roc or Rukh bird from the story of Sinbad the Sailor. The creature did in fact exist. It's scientific name was *Aepyornis jigsaw,* and it lived on Madagascar. Rumours about its legendary presence were rife for centuries. Marco Polo, who never visited Madagascar described a large island where lived a bird so strong that it could lift an elephant. De Flacourt, who commanded a French fort on Madagascar in about 1650, mentions a story, which was in circulation on the island of a gigantic bird which could not be captured because its haunts were so inaccessible. But the most familiar echo of this primitive creature resounds in the Arabian legends of Sinbad the Sailor. The bird must have been about three and a half metres tall and weighed about 500 kilos; a flightless booby, which could not even run very fast. And why should it, for it had no enemies to run away from, except man, of course. After he had discovered the island, about two thousand years ago, the days of the Roc were numbered. The egg of this giant can still be seen in the museums of Cape Town and Aix-en-Provence. It is about thirty centimetres long and, because an egg is always built up out of one single cell, it was the largest living cell ever to have existed. There is also a skeleton of its leg on view in Zürich. It is almost exactly like an ordinary chicken leg, but is two metres long. So this gigantic bird has also disappeared into the depths of history. Only a single tale and a couple of eggs remind us of one of the first species of animals to be exterminated by man.

Scientific Research

Apart from culture, whose network of relationships with nature is overwhelming, nature is used throughout the world as a source of scientific research. This research precedes every use that was and is made of nature. Some 'scientific' (albeit primitive) investigation even preceded the discovery of an edible fruit or an effective medicine in the far distant past. The improvement of agricultural crops, which has been discussed, under 'genetic reserves', comes equally well under scientific research. But let us consider some lesser-known research, whose benefits may one day be economically important.

When Darwin published his work *On the Origin of Species* in 1859, it was extremely controversial, and began a conflict between science and various churches which has not died down even yet. But few people realize that an even more far-reaching Darwinism is now breaking through. As Darwin paved the way for the possibility that man descends physically from the ape, some modern ethologists outline the obvious following step; that his behaviour is also influenced by that of his primitive ancestors. To test this hypothesis, science must turn to the study of animal behaviour. The discoveries made in the meantime have already resulted in Nobel prizes for some research workers occupied with ethology (the study of behaviour), namely Niko Tinbergen, Karl von Frisch and Konrad Lorenz. Much of the knowledge they have gained from studying nature will be of service to the health of man. And here economics comes in.

We have described the need for health as one of the five basic needs. By serving the science of medicine in various ways – as a supplier of ingredients for medicines and as a testing ground for behavioural investigation – nature can provide for these needs. As you might expect a cost-benefit analysis cannot be made here. This is not very serious though. The appreciation of nature's ever-surprising scientific-source function is much more important and is still barely developed.

Nature can also contribute to the well-being of society through research in ecology. An improved understanding of the plants and animals and their relationship with each other and with their environment is important for planning the direction in which society can develop, and for the application of ecological principles to social systems. Through ecology we can understand the way in which natural systems function, how they achieve stability and harmony, how they become thrown off balance and then stabilize again, and which energy and dynamic conditions they have to comply with in order to achieve a certain state.

In searching the professional journals for a theory combining ecology and economics in one system, references to ecological principles can be seen to occur with increasing regularity. But the last word is far from spoken, because these ideas are contrary to one scientific tradition which aims to separate human society from nature, making it unique. This is a line of thought which rejects every ethological and ecological tie we have with nature. Most conservationists regard the tie as a sort of umbilical cord and consider every denial of this principle as unscientific and objectionable.

Recreation

Economic science has been occupied quite exhaustively with the way nature serves recreational needs. This concept is easy to cope with because patterns of recreation can fit into economic theory. By spending their leisure time in a natural area, people express their need for it. From the price they pay one can determine how much the satisfaction of that need by nature is worth to them.

Several methods have been developed for calculating nature's recreation value to people. In each method, attention is paid, for example, to the degree of appreciation of different types of recreation area, the distance people live from it, the way they satisfy their need for recreation elsewhere, and whether they make use of the various provisions in a given recreation area. Details are provided in the official reports which have appeared in the framework of this inquiry. Other important factors include the rarity of the type of area, the number of visitors it has and the expenses they incur in getting there.

Recreation is an industry which has become a prime source of income for many countries, and nature plays a prominent part. Although it cannot be said of the Spanish tourist-coasts that the visitors necessarily go there for nature, on 'our' island, nature is the product which is offered to holiday-makers, just as the corals and flamingos are on Bonaire, the beaches, palms and pines on the Riviera, and the large wild animals in East Africa. Without this product, many of these regions would have little to offer for tourist recreation. Most East African countries would probably never see a single tourist again if it were not for the wild animals.

The economic profit from recreation in nature does not benefit nature itself, of course, but the people who live in its vicinity. Without it, their goods and services would scarcely have any meaning. The danger is that the people who exploit these areas will not realize this, but seek the attraction for their visitors in the goods sold themselves, and not in the presence of forests, estuaries or savannahs and their wild inhabitants. Consequently such areas are often at the mercy of over-exploitation, so that the collective capital is withdrawn from the recreation industry.

In most East African countries, the situation was not like this until a short while ago. In the advertizing of the tourist industry, the presence of game parks was a dominating factor. Because it is realized that they represent a gigantic capital they are usually well-managed. President Mobutu of Zaïre once said, in this connection, 'Nature is our culture. We do not feel inferior because we cannot show our visitors cathedrals or other old monuments or buildings. Nature's is the inseparable and essential element of our specific African character. For this reason, we refuse to follow blindly the path of the 'developed countries' which are aiming at production at any price'.

In Zaïre, a few very large parks, some of which are larger than the entire Netherlands, are now closed off completely from the outside world. No visitor may enter them for the next fifty years. Zambia has laid out 15% of its territory as game reserves, and Tanzania, Kenya and Uganda more than 20%. In these areas, neither agriculture nor any technical development is permitted. Unfortunately, increasingly great herds of cattle, belonging to nomadic tribes, are allowed to graze there. But the old African religions set an example for the reserves. They laid down that the hunting of wild animals was tabu in certain areas. Whenever the animals in other areas were overhunted or exterminated, the population could re-establish itself in these protected regions. There is a similar feeling of ecological consciousness in daily economic practice in many old Third World cultures, and where this conscious-ness has disappeared the reason is very often a poorly planned, overhasty development of Western origin.

This kind of usurpation is much less likely in those countries where people appreciate that the old religious respect for nature can link up very well with modern nature conservation and a flourishing recreation industry. In Kenya, for example, 600,000 foreign visitors brought in the sum of 540 million Kenyan shillings in 1972 (approximately £43 million). The export of coffee brought in 492 million shill-ings, tea 382 million and cotton 24 million. Tourism amoun-ted to 30% of the total, and so formed the single most important export product. About 5% of the working popu-lation in Kenya earns a living from the tourist industry. In Tanzania, tourism accounted for 7% of the total export in 1972, but this share is growing rapidly. By 1975 it had already reached nearly 10%.

It is obvious by now that nature is indispensable for culture. Science, recreation, literature, films and other ex-pressions of art all make use of it. Very often one use is closely interwoven with another. Thus the well-known American, Roger Tory Peterson, has been visiting out-of-the-way corners of the earth for decades to study birds, film, paint and photograph them. He gives lectures on this, writes books and articles and has television stations all over the world showing his films thousands of times a year. His books and obser-vations serve science and promote the recreation of bird-watching. His work has many different economic values but, of course, they reflect only a small part of the value of the birds.

If these birds did not exist, if the wild African animals were not there, if the flamingos of Bonaire were to disappear, and if the dunes on 'our'island did not look so picturesque – in short if the present wealth of nature did not exist – what would then become of science, culture and recreation? How many people would be unemployed, how many books would fail to be written, how many photographs would not be taken, cameras not produced, journeys not be made, hotels not built, aeroplanes not flown, and how many factories would be idle?

Many conservationists make the dangerous error of objecting to this line of reasoning in the same way as Marcuses followers. Both groups point out that people do not really need all those photographs, travels, hotels and aeroplanes, or all the output of industrial production which leads to the destruction of nature and depletion of its resources. Marcuse wants a division into utility and non-utility products. A considerable number of nature conservationists want the same thing, although for a different motive.

The danger of this argument lies in its paternalism. For who should decide what is useful and what is not? Who has the right to decide what people do or do not need? Human needs are as varied as the differences between human beings. If some individuals think they need nature, and other think they need motorbikes, it is impossible to say that one need is real and the other unreal. Anybody who wants this is just asking for Big Brother, who creates order out of chaos. When the need for nature is shown to be perceptible in economic processes, because of all this air travel and so on, it can certainly lead to the deterioration of nature in the long run. But it is simply not true to say that the needs which lead to these consequences are unreal because to some people they may be undesirable. Economic theory does not permit such a division. If the need for nature leads to this kind of industry, then it must be said out loud, calculated and entered in the Gross National Product. There is no point in running away from it.

Fourteen. Towards A Harmony Between Nature and Economics

'If a man gives no thought to what is distant,
he will find sorrow near at hand.'
                                        Confucius

How can one envisage an economic system which no longer considers nature a problem to be overcome, but recognizes the value of its functions and accounts for them?

The science of economics has a simple answer. If people want something from nature, and it is for sale on the market, then the want will be met by the law of supply and demand. If it is *not* for sale, then the government will satisfy the need through political channels. The latter already takes place on a large scale, in the supply and protection of *collective* goods. There may be a demand for them but either they are not marketable goods (such as defence and law and order) or it is thought to be unwise to leave the satisfaction of these requirements to the interplay of demand and supply (or with ignorance and education). For example the need to preserve a variety of cultural values is not generally satisfied by an offering on the market, but by the government's preservation of monuments, provision of museums, and legal protection to landscapes, villages and townscapes, foundation of nature reserves and of services which manage woodlands and landscapes. Likewise, the need for theatre, music and scientific research cannot be left to the free interplay of demand and supply. In these cases the government meets these needs by the *budget-mechanism*.

This is nothing more than a way of distributing the government's gains from tax revenue, in providing for the

good of the community. It is as simple as that. The best way to
fit nature into economics thus seems fairly straightforward; if
it cannot be done through the market-mechanism, then it is
done via the budget-mechanism. If the market does not react,
then the government must. Apparently, no new economic
order is required, for everything seems, in practice, to be
neatly arranged.

Purely theoretically, there is no problem either. Nature fits
existing theories without qualification. These theories teach
us that the aim of economic activity is to alleviate scarcity of
economic commodities and services. People express their
wants in their behaviour. If they find item A more useful than
item B, they choose A. The choice may be from the abundance of goods offered for sale, or of services for which they
have demonstrated a need. So if people think there is a
scarcity of nature, the fact must become obvious from one
signal or other, and an appropriate reaction will follow. By
this theory, nature has only been ignored in the economy up
to now because people have not attributed sufficient usefulness to its functions. And where scarcity does not exist or is
not felt, then neither the market nor the government will
react.

Unfortunately, the theory does not match the reality. For
the theory assumes that people have a complete picture of the
market, and know exactly what is scarce. It has long been
recognized that this is fiction. Neither do people know what
they need. Advertising has grown up to give the people the
necessary information on what is obtainable on the market.
This information however, by definition, is one-sided because it is done on behalf of a firm which wants to sell its
product in competition with others. Especially where little
competition exists, and also where a public enterprise is
dominating the market, the consumer may be given mislead-
ing information and talked into buying something he doesn't
need and which may even be injurious. Therefore advertising
too is subject to various rules and regulations, and consumers
form action groups to keep a close eye on production and
advertising. The free market and the general view of it are

exposed to strong influences which, if all is well, have to counterbalance each other to some extent.

A comparatively new kind of advertising shows how great the need is for nature. With apparently increasing regularity the natural origin of articles is pointed out, or a comparison is made between the article and nature whether selling recreation, relaxation, books, household articles, fruit juices, cosmetics, herbal shampoos or whatever. The advertisers are playing on the need for nature. If that need did not exist then neither would the advertising because it simply would not pay. That nature is misused or misrepresented from time to time is another matter.

It is probable, however, that the need for the many functions of nature we have described is not felt because of ignorance. People do not consciously aim at their own destruction through erosion and despoilation of the natural environment. They achieve it through lack of insight into the importance (including the economic importance) of wildlife.

Economic evaluation of nature does not necessarily have to be expressed in monetary terms. If we establish an order of preference according to purely *ecological* values that is also a kind of *economic* description, because it adds to the knowledge of the 'economic subjects' who have to choose. With the help of this insight, natural goods can be compared with the much-vaunted manufactured goods, and *preference* may be expressed for nature.

One may reproach biologists and nature conservationists for getting no further, in their public support of nature, than saying 'nature is important', that is until recently. Instead they should have worked towards an improved and more widespread understanding of the countless facts which make it so important. Had they done so, it would have brought nature within the scope of economists and decision-makers much sooner. Knowledge of the usefulness, and thus of the economic value of nature, initiates signals – *other* than market signals – of the sort which would make government pay attention to nature. With collective goods already identified as such, there is a precedent set for measures which can be taken by government. The large number of action groups, and the explosive growth of nature-lovers clubs, together with the new elements of the need for nature and a better environment, is yet another signal. In many countries, this signal has resulted in *some* reactions and corrections on the part of the government.

For economists, the theory stops here, because it is impossible to say beforehand how significant these signals are. One can only deduce this information from the political reactions of the government, and then only after the event, because, on the basis of what the government decides, it is obvious which alternatives were *not* chosen. If, for example, the government decides against turning a certain natural area into a harbour, then they clearly attach more value to the continued existence of that chunk of nature than to the future yields from the harbour – as calculated at that moment. If this decision has been made after political pressure from the public, then this has led to a kind of preference signal, because the piece of nature concerned is, ultimately, *implicitly* valued at a sum greater than the expected harbour yields.

So it seems that there are ever-increasing difficulties with the market- and budget-mechanism theory. In times of plenty, of great growth of production, little unemployment and good trade relations, a place for nature is readily found. People are more easily inclined then to make delicate gradations in the concept 'economic growth', including combating the scarcity of nature. But if production has slowed down, if the unemployed become impatient, inflation out of hand and the future dark, this understanding quickly fades. The lonely environmental-economist shrugs his shoulders at the stupidity of a public which in the emergency has turned its back on nature once more in favour of the doubtful benefit expected from a new wave of production.

But there is apparently something wrong with the theory that only wishes to bring the consideration of nature within current economic activities. At least, that is the only way to explain why, when it comes to it, the public is simply not interested and returns to its old ways. The missing link is this: production growth was intended in the first place for the acquisition of goods and prosperity. This has certainly succeeded in Western industrial countries. A whole fairground of social structures, bastions almost, has grown up around production, in which the money earned is transferred, deposited, accumulated, sold, merged, invested in funds and paid out in interest. There are banks, stock exchanges, superannuation schemes, insurance schemes and governments with a far-reaching system of social provision. This entire cobweb, which is called the *transfer sector*, is suspended by all its threads from production. Most people feel that this web threatens to become detached, either of its own accord, or because of the need for nature, particularly now for example, when industry is stagnating. Thus, the economic theory has become overshadowed by a world-wide *financial* (and not *economic*) system of agreements which it has created but which has become an end in itself.

Through its enormous mass, the transfer sector works like a flywheel trying to keep on turning. So the goal of economy has shifted. The primary aim of production is no longer to overcome poverty, but it seems that production must be continued at any price for the sake of keeping the financial system intact. Accompanying this is a widespread conviction that the only way to keep the system going is by increasing production. In Western industrial countries this notion is fixed as immovably as a pile in the ground and the popular belief 'Standstill is recession' has been elevated to the axiom of production. As soon as growth falls off, the community is in an uproar. Therefore, in spite of all the theories about scarcity of nature, production will continue, with a growth rate of 3%, 5% or 7% per annum as necessary, which will irrevocably lead to the destruction of nature all over the world. A little earlier here, a little later there, but it will be destroyed.

Prosperity does not increase if the environment which brings it falls victim to production. And in most industrial countries nowadays, a growing part of production consists of apparatus to clean up the environment, clear away rubbish and protect nature. More often than not this is by way of repairing the damage caused by production's negative external effects. This important aspect can be called 'repair or recovery production'. Repair or recovery, that is, of a state which should have been maintained, but which has suffered through mismanagement. In the economy, as with so many other repairs, this is entered up as *production*, i.e. as *income*. But in fact it is *expenditure*, just as the repair of a gutter is entered as expenditure in the housekeeping book.

Anyone who makes this kind of mistake also invites inflation in. For all these repairs call for the laying in of labour and capital, which must be paid and made to pay. As a rule, the costs will not be recoverable from those who caused the damage and who profit from it by passing on the expense in the price of the product. That means this payment must be met by the nation. An increase in government expenditure does not necessarily mean inflation if, at least, it is possible to call on labour *which has not been previously used* or on production capacity *which is still attainable*. If, however, *both* of these are fully occupied, and no reduction in the use of goods or services from their capacity is required, then these repair activities will have to compete with existing production. This is what leads to price increases and inflation.

The truth that people must start to realize is that present production is too cheap, because it does not bear the costs of the damage it causes. If this were done the costs would have to be passed on to the public.

With present calculating methods, anyone who does not to some degree preserve the natural environment by controlling his effect on it, but causes damage and tries to obviate it by technological means, runs the risk of advancing the time when the expenditure of an economy is greater than its income. For these reasons, a healthy economy must go hand in hand with the optimal control of nature.

No matter how significant the short-term effect of nature's purification may be, if capital investments in this quarter cannot be passed on in the price of the product, they will aggravate the likelihood of a fall in the value of money. But these are not the only reasons why nature conservationists plead so often for lower capital intensity in production, for another use of capital or for small-scale initiatives; there is a further important motive, which some ecologists have pointed out. The capital needed to keep production up to the mark in ever-diminishing returns. At one time, you pushed a curtain-rod into the ground and black gold (oil) came out. Now you have to put gold into the ground to get the last remains of oil out. More and more capital seems to be needed to develop more and more inaccessible sources of energy and raw materials. And more energy is needed to obtain energy.

The same diminishing returns can be seen in food production. Harvests cannot keep on growing by putting more money (artificial fertilizer, machines, pesticides) into the ground. The same applies to fisheries. Larger investments, and bigger ships, bring about a decrease in yields instead of an increase, because the fish are being exterminated. Whether fisheries, food production or energy, it is the same old song: more money goes in, but relatively less comes back. *So the money is worth less.*

The 'steady state'

From all the information, it seems that the community is forced to accept an *upper limit*, beyond which it may not and cannot grow any further. If it tries to grow more, the result is destruction of nature, inflation, disruption of the economy and therefore of the entire social system. Consequently, the need is created to *stabilize* production at a certain level and to set up a *steady state* or stable *economy*. Dennis Gabor calls this *mature* economy, a final goal of growth which John Stuart Mill considered desirable.

In nature, the steady state is called a climax system, that is, a state in which the processes, cycles and structures are *constant*. There are many activities or fluctuations, but they produce a fairly constant average. What goes into the system comes out again, and vice versa. This kind of system exhibits

a large degree of immunity to sudden changes (the homeo-
stasis) and those changes which do take place are attuned to
each other. So there is an equilibrium between coming into
being, growth and death. In ecology this steady state, the
highest natural state of system development, is called *mature*.
It is the final stage of growth.

In practice, the interweaving of the *natural* steady state and
the social dependence on it are disturbed by the addition of
much *energy* to human organization. Large energy flows help
to loosen the ties with the natural environment, and create the
impression that any dependence is definitely at an end.

This notion can only stand if we assume that there is no
autonomous feed-back reaction from nature to our social
system; in other words, that our enormous energy flows allow
us finally to sever the human life-line to nature. In practice we
can gain no lead over her.

By inference, the more people use the natural system and,
above all, the more energy they consume in doing so, the
faster it deteriorates in bearing-power and quality. History
teaches us that this ultimately brings the downfall of the
population itself. It is by the use of technology and such vast
amounts of energy that modern man has succeeded in
postponing this downfall. But increasing use of energy
simultaneously shifts the problems further away in time and
makes them more serious, as the social system becomes more
vulnerable. Vulnerable, because supplies and conditions in
an energy-intensive system are 'techno-synthetic' instead of
being integrated with the natural environment. The discon-
nection of this technological supply means a laborious re-
adaptation to the natural environment.

The obvious way to obtain a more durable relationship
with the remaining natural environment seems to be by
stabilizing growth. The environment is then given an opportunity to stabilize itself again.

A steady-state economy must be based on *natural laws* and
ethical principles. These natural laws include those of thermodynamics (science of heat) and the ecological theories
connected with them. They indicate the limits of the extent to

which man can exploit nature and its resources.

The *ethical* problems start off with this question: how many people can be made happy if the cake they have to share does not keep on growing, and how livable will the world be then? But first, how do the rules of *economics*, the *laws of nature* and the *ethical* principles of the steady state link up with each other?

A steady state economy is planned so that the supplies of the goods of prosperity (all those things – including natural things which make life pleasant) are *constant* with a *constant* population. The level at which these stores acquire a constant value is *chosen* and not imposed by a compulsory system, neither by dictator nor by hunger, for example. The *free flow* in this system is small, i.e. birth and death rates are low and balance one another. The volume of energy-intensive production is small and the flow of waste inconsiderable. But the durability of the commodities is great. Compared with today, the labour intensity of production has greatly increased again. Because solar energy is the only source which improves the system, both ecologically and physically, the economy hinges on solar energy, including derived forms, such as wind, tides and hydrogen gas. And the energy is chiefly used for maintaining the high-quality and durable character of the economy. The services sector has been greatly extended, as well as the cultural and educational sectors, although there is still room for growth, if people want it.

Compare this economy with the ecological climax system: it is both stable and varied, and well able to cope with changing influences. One can also measure the extent to which the steady state has been achieved on the basis of *use of natural resources* which, at the moment, is more in keeping with the familiar relationships of production. The use of these resources must remain more or less constant, as happens already with all those sophisticated technological products, which have the same function as their massively-constructed predecessors, but which are produced and work with a minimal use of raw materials. A modern computer is a good example. The article is very small, durable, and achieves

as much as, or even more than, its predecessor of twenty years
ago, which was hundreds of times larger and also required
just as many resources. However, resource-saving growth
is finite, because there comes a point at which one can go
no further in making something more economical, finer,
smaller or more durable.

The present craze for insulating dwellings is a good
example of the type of production which may keep on
growing for a while within the rules of the steady state, but
this refinement too will reach its limits when all houses have
been insulated, and no improvements in insulation are
possible. Just as in a climax vegetation, there is a great deal of
movement in the steady-state economy, for it is a dynamic
system. In this economy too, personal development and
interest is encouraged; there is industry, there is production,
so the sorely-feared 'stagnation' is avoided.

The problems of the laws of nature hinge on the question of
whether human activities have much or little influence on the
biosphere as a whole. If the effects are great obviously there is
a problem. If they are slight, and in keeping with the
absorption capacity of the biosphere, then there is nothing
wrong. Wrongly, in our opinion. For, if only from the yards-
long list of exterminated and threatened species of plants and
animals, from the speed at which the deserts are advancing
and the primeval forests are being swept away, from oceanic
pollution and from the climatological disturbances which are
now minimal but will be drastic in the long run, it is easy to
see that human activity can have world-embracing effect.
When, on the one hand, world population increases, and on
the other hand, the quality of the biosphere and with it the
possibility of finding a reasonable existence decreases because
of all our activities, things are going wrong. The questions of
whether the biosphere is indeed 'degrading', and so offering
less expectation of life, is therefore of the utmost importance.

Entropy

In this connection, the world 'entropy' has been cropping up in the literature of more enlightened economists in recent years. It is a rather complicated concept derived from the science of thermodynamics. The second principle law of thermodynamics (the law of the conservation of energy), teaches us that all processes in a closed system result in 'disorder' or a decrease in the 'order' of the material in that system. This use of the terms order and disorder can perhaps best be explained by seeing the earth as a closed system, with the sun as the only factor exercizing influence on it from outside. A fixed quantity of raw materials is present in the system, and the living things have to use them in some way in order to stay alive. Before we can use these raw materials, they have to be assimilated into organic matter, concentrated and subsequently converted into products. The fixing of materials to make them fit for use begins in nature with photosynthesis. Here, a process of growth is started off, so that solar energy and nutrients become *concentrated*. Thermodynamics uses the term *ordering*, or negative entropy. Non-organic, (i.e. dead) matter, can also be looked on as 'order' when appearing in concentrated form in minerals.

If we refer to production, the second law of thermodynamics says that the ultimate result of this process will be a decrease of order and an increase of disorder; that is, an increase of entropy. On the face of it, one would say that when man is producing something, he is ordering affairs. For the process of production involves raw materials being taken, graded and processed. However, this law states that the waste materials and heat produced during these production processes create more disorder than the production itself creates order. Only the natural process, in which solar energy is fixed through photosynthesis, results in an increase of order, in spite of the heat given off by plants through respiration. All other production processes lead to disorder, so the final result is great disorder, measurable in the disturbed heat balance of the planet. This measurement shows more clearly than any graduator whether the biosphere, as a whole, is decreasing in productive capacity. This is because a disturbed heat balance has unimaginably great consequences for the climate, and thus for the existence of life. Even an increase less than one per cent is enough to create this disturbance.

This entropy theory makes it clear that we can rule out the possibility of maintaining a durable, high-quality economy if it is not based on the need to reduce heat production as far as possible. In practice, every energy source inimical to the biosphere is tabu. The only motive power on which the economy should turn is that which the sun supplies and is converted into usable energy and matter. This means that only the interest of the natural capital may be used, and that the community must aim to increase this capital, consolidate it and improve the way in which its fruits are plucked. If we do not, increased production will cause greater disorder, only to be combated by supplies of more and more deleterious energy. This will lead to a further increase in disorder; and so it goes on, in a negative spiral which we know as 'the law of the conservation of misery'.

Originally, the entropy concept was only used in physics, but because it is so apposite, its use has spread to other fields even though the application is not quite correct. Thus, the term 'social entropy', is used to illustrate how the activities of a community, which ought to create order, somehow result in disorder. One example is a large bureaucratic organisation, such as the British National Health Service, whose number of civil servants increased by 1200% within ten years, while the speed at which a form circulated through that bureaucracy dropped from three weeks to over a year. More people, more organization, more 'social energy' going into the system, the less order as a result. This is 'social entropy', and the principle is of more importance for nature conservationists than they may imagine. For, in most industrial countries, the assaults on nature are the product of a steady increase in technological machinery, the idea being that order is created by these activities, whereas often the reverse is true. We all know the road-widening phenomenon, carried out in order to improve the traffic flow. The widened road then attracts more traffic, is again found to be too narrow and is widened once more. In various parts of the world, this has already resulted in cities which are little more than one vast traffic circuit. In other words, the entropy of the technological community tends to keep on growing, not only in the sense used in natural science but also in a social sense. What is urgently needed is a study of this theory's consequences in order to find the best way of measuring the retrogression of the social and biological systems, so that more appropriate steps may be taken.

For the practically-minded economist and technologist, all this means that the only correct source of energy for the future is the sun, including the wind, water and tidal power derived from it. It also means that the re-use (recycling) of raw materials is a necessity because this way, in spite of the marginal losses and energy use, the world's natural resources acquire a *flow* character.

Besides these technical and physical aspects, there is an ethical problem attached to. the steady-state economy for, even though the conditions for a steady-state may be complied with – i.e. a constant stream of goods with a constant level of solar energy and population – the problem then is how to allocate the supplies because the total amount available is finite.

Growth of production

In recent times, increased production has helped to solve many problems and should still be able to do so (and may have to) in many countries. The desire to increase production comes not only from the belief in progress, but also from something as worldly as a bulkier wage packet. If production increases, the income rises with it, and everyone can earn more each year. In this system, the existing differences in income do not need to be quibbled over. However, if the size of the cake remains the same every year, there are two possibilities: either the existing distribution of income, whereby everyone receives (or fails to receive) a certain portion of the cake, is just and politically attainable, or the old custom of promising more and more persists and, while it is still possible, is taken away from those who had the larger share of the cake. With the latter people sell each other the illusion that there is more to gain than there is, resulting in a pseudo-growth, which is actually inflation. Obviously in a steady-state economy, the transfer-sector also comes into its own. Anyone who stabilizes at the level of 1970, for example (a purely random choice), can check how large the flow of goods was in that year, how high the level of supplies and how well the financial 'cobweb' adhered to production. But he can also check that, under those stable conditions, any possibilities of greatly improving incomes is estimated. Anyone offering more will have to produce a working prescription for the division of incomes on more equal terms. Inevitably it will be short-lived.

Most conservationists, notably the older, great pioneers among them, cannot comprehend this conclusion, because they do not associate it with the theory of steady state as nature's friend, but with radical political demands. This is a misapprehension, for people will have to realize that no dream economy can exist, growing in the old way and at the same time preserving nature. When nature conservation entered officialdom about seventy years ago, this wish seemed feasible but, as we have learned in the past few years how great the connection is between conservation, expansion of production, population growth and energy level, no right-minded nature conservationist would deny the next step we envisage. Nature conservation, the steady state, the unalterable cake, the division of incomes and the division of work still available – these are great moves on one board. There is not one bit of radicalism. But some new questions immediately arise such as what is the employment situation in the steady state economy?

The enormous increase in production in recent decades was made possible by a drastic replacement of labour by capital. Where a hundred workers were once needed, they have been replaced by a single piece of machinery, operated by one skilled technician. The investment for that situation is very large, and the yield is correspondingly great. It is a favourable state for those who furnish the capital, and of course also for the remaining employee, who is quite well off. Many of those who were made redundant have moved into the services sector. Some of them people offices and government agencies, and also receive reasonable salaries, because the economy there hinges on the same kind of high-grade capital goods as the technological marvel which previously replaced them. There is so much income that a large part is left for paying an extensive services sector which, in its turn, has enough purchasing power to keep the production of the private sector up to scratch. However, some of the redundant employees will not find new jobs, because the capital, technological ingenuity and commercial resourcefulness were unable to create new machines with equally high yield. The jobs are simply not available.

In the view of most economists, this was merely a temporary problem, until recently: we had only to exercise a little patience, and the gap would be filled. Technology stops at nothing! The increasing unemployment, they said, was only a trend. Should the business outlook change for the better, through technology's intervention, and the whole cycle enter a more congenial phase, the worst of the unemployment will soon be over. But recently they have come to realize that there is more to the problem and accept the existence of 'structural' employment. Those who have capital will obviously continue replacing labour with it as long as it pays them to do so, because experience shows this leads to a relatively higher output. Therefore more and more mammoth tankers are being built, with increasingly sophisticated technology and needing far smaller crews. Factories too are becoming more and more complex producing more with fewer workers. And if wage demands rise, it will only tighten this spiral.

Remarkably, in this continuous replacement of labour by capital, the growth of technological ingenuity, which makes the process possible, is regarded as an inevitable constant. Not surprisingly this is sometimes depressing for the community, like the force of destiny. The common notion is that if our country dropped out of this rat-race, others would not,

and we would then 'fall behind'. If we wanted to escape from
the treadmill for the sake of nature conservation and try to
achieve a stable level of production and energy, and a
replacement of capital by labour, it would all be impossible
because other countries would then 'out-trade' us. This belief
is generally held – but nonetheless foolish.

The primary aim of production is *not* to keep up with
foreign countries but to maintain a *desirable level of prosperity*.
If that prosperity is threatened by unemployment, over-
production and environmental pollution, then the measures
we advocate must be taken to counteract this threat. They are
then desired – more so than the standard of foreign countries
– merely to accomplish one's own interpretation of 'prosperity'. If people decide to replace capital with labour, and
so on, that is the result of a social process rooted in people's
genuine wishes. While labour intensiveness may mean lower
comparative income this is acceptable in a stable economy.

The absolute valuation of income, 'more is better', is then
replaced by a relative, 'less is better', valuation, for that leads
to more employment and to less spoilation of the environment
and of nature. In addition, this attitude is rooted in a better
understanding of the true meaning of the phenomenon
income. Income is a claim on desired, scarce goods. There is
no meaning in money itself, but only what you can do with it.
Someone who lives in a wood has an income of peace, quiet,
nature, fresh air and relaxation, requiring no financial outlay.
A man living in a city, and with the same needs, has to have an
income in money to obtain these same pleasures. The more
money you have, the more you can buy; and even nature is
expensive. For, before you can get to that wood, you need a
means of transport, enough free time and the means to pay for
it all. Unfortunately for the rich, you can't buy most natural
things so easily.

Employment is not for sale either. Renouncing the technological spiral will lead to a *fall* in the amount of cash for
spending, but also to an *increased* availability of scarce
'goods', such as nature or suitable work. This is sometimes
called the *immaterial* income, as distinct from the material

income, which is money. We feel the distinction is incorrect however, as there is actually no difference between the type of pleasure bought with money, and the type obtained naturally. Both forms of income are identical in the long run.

The effect of all these measures is that while the position with regard to other countries changes, it does not deteriorate. It is hardly serious. The employment and prosperity the people want will have been reached and, while wages will have become low compared with other countries, the trading position will be influenced in a different way. This seems the only path open for overcrowded industrial countries, unless they are really bent on self-destruction.

This is a book about facts, not dreams. We know that the true world situation gives no cause for optimism that the theories we promote might soon be applied. The compulsion to persist with the current growth of production appears so strong that people will go to any lengths to continue with it. There is still no question of any voluntary limitation, and developed countries show little sign of being willing to reduce to the 'standard of living' of the rest of the world, even in the framework of a steady-state economy. For they automatically, but erroneously, associate such a change with less of social pleasures. Even the wish that more sciences, such as ecology should be considered in economic policy-making seems too much to ask. Had this small concession been granted it might already have prevented a great deal of distress. An obvious correction of the GNP has not been made either, though people have requested this for years.

Economists and politicians are not the only ones to be blamed, however. Conservationists also will have to go much further in working out the ultimate consequences of their aims. Nature conservationists often profess that they, more than other people, have some understanding of how complex and vulnerable is the network of life on earth. They must make use of that advantage by helping to unravel the political, social and psychological consequences of their objectives.

In the past fourteen years the world population has risen from 3,000 million to 4,000 million. The next 1,000 million may take only eleven years. If the present rate of production and world population continues, there will be ever-growing encroachment on the remains of nature. This will reduce the carrying capacity of the biosphere. Inevitably great political and social tensions will result, because there are more and more people, who have less and less to expect from the natural environment.

Nature conservationists are the defenders of the biosphere. They must stand in the full glow of the public floodlights and state that nature has its limits. They will have to mobilize economists and specialists in other fields to help people with the painful process of adapting themselves to the restraints of what remains. Nature can hit back hard and cruelly. It has happened all too often in history. Luckily, we still have some chance of preventing a recurrence. But we cannot afford to be complacent.

Fifteen. Back to the Island

'We are surrounded and embraced by her.
Unasked and without warning, she takes us
up in the circle of her dance.'
                    Goethe in *Die Natur*

Perhaps one day, a community with the kind of economy described in this book will really exist. This seems like wishful thinking, especially since the necessary changes do seem rather drastic. True enough. But, in practice, great economic changes do take place gradually and imperceptibly. Only at the end of the series does the extent of the alterations become obvious. It is like a sailor still far out at sea, who decides not to head for the lighthouse but for the other end of the island. Just a small turn of the helm is enough change for him to arrive at a totally different spot.

So, in the economy no very drastic restrictions are needed to end up with a considerable change in the community. Energy plays a key role in this change. The longer cheap energy is available, the longer it will take before the restrictions make themselves felt because, with the help of cheap energy, technical artifices can disguise the way natural capital is being exhausted. If that situation is ended, the economy will gradually adjust itself. But the more one depends on energy, the more difficult it is to adjust.

Looking back to the island, what can we hope will have happened twenty years from now . . .. The economic-ecological relationships have become harmonious, and cemented with the passing of time. The growth of production (meaning the growth of the recreation industry) has come to a halt, and is organized to perfection. Too perfectly, perhaps, but it could hardly be otherwise. To begin with, a strict maximum limit to the number of visitors has been laid down. In the first few years, this led to many protests, since neither the tourist industry nor the holiday-makers would stand for any restrictions, and they looked on government intervention as interference with the freedom of the individual. But, gradually that attitude changed, especially when people started to see more clearly just how comparative that freedom really was: freedom to drive round a limited network of roads with too many cars, to obstruct cyclists and pedestrians, pollute the air and scare birds away. Freedom to disturb the peace with motorcycles and mopeds and rouse people from their sleep. Freedom to open new shops, hotels and boarding houses, so that the quantity kept on growing but the quality became inferior. For with all that competition, the main object was the number of tourists and the amount of money and no longer the quality of the product being sold, which had traditionally consisted of nature and peace. There was freedom also to attack nature and fritter away the collective capital.

Things went 'well' for some years. Ever-increasing streams of tourists came along and nobody had a care in the world. Then a series of rainy, chilly summers knocked the bottom out of the business. The island lost its almost southern atmosphere, and the customers stayed away – they went to the real South. In earlier years, the island would ride out these bad summers because the visitors then did not mind a little rain and wind; they came for The Product – the beautiful landscape and the friendly local culture. But The Product deteriorated as mass tourism sprang up; the island lost its specific value and its big sales point. This was certainly brought home to the inhabitants. Years of great recession resulted and the people had time to reflect on the reasons. They quickly realized that their recent wealth came from a bogus income obtained from consuming the natural assets. It was an unforgivable mistake, which every book-keeper, housewife or administrator can understand, but which nobody had wanted to acknowledge in those days of deceptive wealth. But they have learned from their mistake and the apparent freedom of former days has had to make way for the voluntary limitation of the numbers of tourists, cars, roads, bungalows, hotels, camping sites, cafes and souvenir shops.

What many people had feared most was that, with a stable economy, there would be nothing more to occupy them, that apathy would prevail and every challenge would disappear. But experience on the island has proved the fear ill-founded for it is a hive of activity. Its economy is a 'maintenance economy', whose aim is to maintain the natural and cultural capital in their present healthy condition.

There is nothing new however. There are building contractors, plumbers and painters, farmers, foresters and bird-watchers, hotel keepers and publicans, and bus drivers. The difference is that these tradespeople no longer have the right or the motive to continually expand their collective business from year to year. No longer is there an annual toll exacted from the vegetation, the space, the quiet and the clean air for the sake of extra profit. Anyone who wants to expand his business has to do so at the expense of others. And that is enough inducement for people to keep their businesses and surroundings in first-class condition, because if they become slovenly it gives the advantage to their competitors in the market. It is still a free and competitive economy, but problems arising cannot be solved by the classical method of growth, just by giving everyone his due share of what is constantly available. Everybody knows this, so as years go by competition is not achieved by mere expansion but by improvement in quality and efficiency. At one time, it even seemed as if there was room for some old-fashioned growth, because improvements in applied technology, and increased efficiency naturally allow a better use of production methods. This is especially true for those who produce better results, because of their training and greater understanding of the relationship with the natural environment. But because of their comprehension the new way prevailed. It is also true, though, when comparing prices and incomes in the rest of the economy, where people are still 'lagging behind', and which contrast unfavourably with the level on the island. The advantages for the islanders lies in shorter working hours or greater pleasure in work, and in this way they are more prosperous.

The development of agriculture on the island is particularly interesting. Like other businessmen, the farmers have had to alter their methods to avoid the destruction of their capital and that meant restrictions on the use of artificial fertilizer, pesticides and intensive systems of livestock husbandry. It also meant some degree of management of the natural elements around the farm, such as thickets, hedges, and ditches of water. And the farmer's income is derived from managing both his own fields and the surrounding nature. A mixture of agricultural science and experience has come up with the best breeds and methods to give the highest possible yields under these conditions, and high-quality products with a ready market.

At one time people thought it ridiculous to crave for the return of the draught-horse, but it has long since been obvious that the costs of this solar-energy horse-power (sun-grass-horse) are much lower than those of the energy from oil, the use of which is now declining all over the island. With the new economy comes a limit to the ground available for cultivation, so that the island now has about thirty large farms. They are up-to-date, with rich vegetation and surrounded by dense 'ecological' reservoirs. They are modern farms in every sense, where nature is better understood than ever before on a farm, where wind and solar energy are used, and where some mixed farming goes on, because some arable land for one's own use increases the diversity and thus the stability.

Little by little, the cultural interest too has returned to the island. It has been described before, for example in *The Blueprint for Survival* (1972), *Limits to Growth* (1972) and *A Time to Choose* (1974). There it was worked out, in rather an abstract manner, that the harmony between people in a steady state would be much greater than in an expansion economy, in which everyone is fighting for more. But on the island,

those old model calculations have proved to be true. Nervous
strain has disappeared from people's lives, and anyone who
wants interests outside his daily employment turns to the
time-honoured, socio-cultural activities, of which there are
many hundreds in every community. And although they are
neglected in an expanding economy they are valued in a
steady state.

Does this mean a step back to the old days? To cold, hunger
and lack of comfort? Not at all: the reverse, in fact. The
economy was stabilized at a voluntarily-chosen level of
production, that of 1965, which means that conditions of
food, housing, warmth, prosperity and so forth, are good.
People do not make such decisions to become less prosperous,
but to become more so. For choosing 1965 is a better
alternative than falling back to the level of 1918, for example,
which would have been the result if unbridled growth had
continued. The difference between now and the 1960s is that
people take better care of nature's needs and of the social and
cultural needs of the community. In addition there is always
the necessity of renovations, which can satisfy inventiveness
and curiosity. For the steady state economy exists by the
grace of a technology compatible with nature, and calls for a
technological refinement and ingenuity which demand all
possible attention and creativity. Now that solar energy
systems can be obtained all over the world and, unlike the
1970s, have become economical, building them no longer
presents a problem, any more than the new windmill power
stations, a series of which have been erected on a large
sandbank to the west of the island, to supply all the energy
required. In this sense, there is growth, because for years now
companies have been busy installing these natural energy
systems, insulating houses and using improved methods of
heat storage.

Abstract theorists say that this economy works on the
'negative entropy' principle, and that seems to make them
happy. The term is used to denote the arrangement whereby
the irradiated solar energy (and, of course, the nature which
depends on it) is converted into economic order and pro-

sperity without creating 'disorder'. The abstract belief is that 'disorder' results only from using energy that is not fresh from the sun, such as fossil and nuclear energy. But why should the islanders or tourists care? They are enjoying the benefits of the restored Product – a nature which is left alone to grow richer every year, and an island where one can really relax.

The island has rather led the way in these developments, because the limitations of the old economy became visible very early on. No wonder: sea transport costs were high and possibilities for expansion small, because the sea is a permanent barrier. So when the new developments started, technicians and scientists from all over the world came to watch the economic-ecological scale model evolving. It started in 1974, and is still going on.

When you stand on the most westerly dunes in the evening and see the forest of masts on great, vertical windmills, looking like so many mixers, what a strange and ugly sight that is. At one time this spot was deserted and silent. Now the air is filled with a high-pitched hum, vaguely reminiscent of the sound from the sails of the old corn mills as they swept round. The mature economy is not always nature's idea of beauty, and this enormous wind-power station is monstrous. But the price is well-worth paying. Behind us, the island lies in the falling dusk. But we nature conservationists are still not satisfied for, if we did not know better, it would seem as if little had changed. A terrific hullabaloo is coming from the village at the foot of the dune. Holiday makers in festive mood, returning from a covered waggon trip to the nature reserve. Can't things be just a little quieter in the mature economy? People are recovering from a century of expansion, and surely it should be celebrated in suitable silence. But no, people don't fit in with the dreams of the naturalist and his high ideals.

A great gaggle of geese flies over in a long V shape. When we come down from the dune, out of earshot of the noisy merrymaking, we hear the curious cackling of the geese, which drown the swishing of the windmills.

Geese – just as in the old days: not so very much has changed after all, except that they fly over in greater numbers now, and more often. Nature is recovering from a great relapse. Here, on the island, you can see that very clearly. ... We only hope it happens.

Bibliography

Allen, R., 'Saving wetlands for a rainy day', in *New Scientist* 68
(1975) nr. 980.
Arthur, D. e.a., 'A blueprint for survival', in *The Ecologist* 2
(1972) nr. 1.
Bates, M., *The forest and the sea*, New York, 1961.
Boulding, K., 'The economics of the coming Space Ship Earth',
in *Environmental Quality in a Growing Economy*, Baltimore, 1966.
idem, *The economics of love and fear*, Wadsworth, Californië, 1973.
Broecker, W. S., 'Man's oxygen reserves', in *Science* 168 (1970),
p. 1537/38.
Colinveaux, P. A., *Introduction to ecology*, New York, 1973.
Crawford, M. A. & S. M. Crawford, *An examination of new sys-
tems of livestock management based on African ecosystems*, London,
1971.
Daly, H., *Towards a Steady State Economy*, New Orleans, 1972.
Deutsch, J. J., 'How did we get into this mess?', in *The Globe
and Mail*, 16 nov. 1974.
Development Forum, 'Fisheries, a resource resource', *Action
UNDP* 2 (1974) nr. 7.
Dorst, J., *Avant que la nature meure*, Neuchatel, 1965.
Ehrlich, P. R. & A. H. Ehrlich, *Population, resources, environment*,
San Francisco, 1970.
Everett, T. H., *Living trees of the world*, New York, 1966.
Frankel, O. H. & E. Bennet, *Genetic resources in plants – their ex-
ploration and conservation*, Londen, 1970.
Freeman, D. e.a., *A time to choose*, Ford Foundation Energy
Policy Project, Washington, 1974.
Gabor, D., *Progress report working party of the Club of Rome*, juli
1973.
idem, 'The transition to mature society', in *TED-Tijdschrift voor
Efficient Directiebeleid* 44 (1974) nr. 7, p. 222/229.

Georgescu Roegen, N. G., *The entropy law and the economic process*, Cambridge, Mass., 1971.

Goodland, R. J. A. & H. S. Irwin, *An ecological discussion of the environmental impact of the highway construction programm in the Amazone Basin.*

Heilbroner, R. L., *The prospect of man*, New York, 1974.

Henderson, H., 'The coming economic transition', in *Technological Forecasting and Social Change*, 8-1976.

idem, 'The entropy state', in *Planning Review*, mei 1974.

Henriquez, P. C., 'Development aid and world ecology', in *International Spectator*, 8-11-1967.

Hueting, R., *Wat is de natuur ons waard?*, Baarn, 1970.

Hueting, R., *Nieuwe schaarste en economische groei*, Amsterdam, 1974.

Longman, K. A. & J. Jenik, *Tropical forest and its environment*, Londen, 1974.

Maslov, A. H., *Motivation and personality*, New York, 1970.

Meadows, D. L. e.a., *Towards global equilibrium*, Cambridge, Mass., 1973.

Melle, G. van, 'Wildlife utilization', in *Intermediair* 11 (1975) nr. 3.

Mishan, E., *The costs of economic growth*, Londen, 1967.

idem, 'The economics of hope', in *The Ecologist* 1 (1971) nr. 1.

Mörzer Bruyns, M. F., 'The importance of the Wadden area as a natural area, both nationally and internationally' in *A plea for the Wadden Sea*, Utrecht, 1966.

Mörzer Bruyns, W. F. J., 'Whales', in *Nature in Focus*, nr. 17, 1973.

Odum, E. P., 'The stategy of ecosystem development', in *Science* 164 (1969) p. 262–270.

idem, *Fundamentals of ecology*, Philadelphia, 1974.

idem, *The value of the tidal marsh*, Baton Rouge, 1973.

Odum, H. T., *Environment, power and society*, New York, 1971.

Rooth, J., *The flamingos of Bonaire*, Utrecht, 1975.

Saint Marc, Ph., *Socialisation de la nature*, Parijs, 1971.

Schumacher, E. F., *Small is beautiful*, New York, 1973.

Steinbeck, J., *The grapes of wrath*, Middlesex, 1959.

'Study on Critical Environmental Problems', in *Man's impact on the global environment*, Cambridge, Mass., 1971.

Talbot, L. M., 'Comparison of the efficiency of wild animals and domestic livestock in utilization of East African range-lands', in *IUCN N.S.* 1 : 329–35, 1963.

Thijsse, Jac. P., *Will Java become a desert?*, Den Haag, 1975.

United Nations, *Statistical handbook* 25–1969.

Vermeulen, F. E., *Terschelling* 1900–1975, Wageningen, 1975.

Vries, E. de, *Maintenance of productivity of tropical soils*, Pittsburg, 1975.

Zijlstra, J. J., 'On the importance of the Waddensea as a nursery area in the relation to the conservation of the southern North Sea fishery resources', *Symposium Zoological Society London* (1972) nr. 29, 233–258.